EMERGENCY COMMUNICATION FOR PREPPERS

A Guide to be Connected With Family Members and Receive Information During Disaster

CHADWICK FREDERICK COLE

Copyright © 2024 by Chadwick Frederick Cole

All rights reserved. No part of this publication may be reproduced, distributed, or transmitted in any form or by any means, including photocopying, recording, or other electronic or mechanical methods, without the prior written permission of the publisher, except in the case of brief quotations embodied in critical reviews and certain other noncommercial uses permitted by copyright law.

Table of Contents

Table of Contents   2
INTRODUCTION   1
   The Importance of Emergency Communication 1
CHAPTER 1   9
Understanding the Basics of Emergency Communication   9
   What is Emergency Communication?   9
   Why Communication Fails During Disaster   19
   Different Types of Communication Methods   29
CHAPTER 2   41
Preparing Your Communication Plan   41
   Identifying Communication Needs for Your Family   41
   Setting Up a Communication Tree   51
   Developing a Family Emergency Communication Plan   61
CHAPTER 3   73
Tools and Technologies for Emergency Communication   73
   Handheld Radios   73
   Satellite Phones: Pros and Cons   83
   Mobile Apps and Online Platforms for Emergency Use   93
CHAPTER 4   105
Setting Up a Home Communication Hub   105
   Choosing the Right Equipment for Your Hub 105
   Powering Your Communication Devices   116
   Securing Your Communication Hub from Cyber

Threats　　127
CHAPTER 5　　**141**
Establishing Communication Protocols　　**141**
　　Code Words and Signals for Security and Clarity　　141
　　When and How to Use Emergency Frequencies　　151
　　Communicating Under Stress　　162
CHAPTER 6　　**175**
Staying Informed: Receiving Emergency Alerts and Updates　　**175**
　　Understanding Emergency Alert Systems (EAS)　　175
　　NOAA Weather Radios and Their Importance　　186
　　Utilizing Local Networks and Social Media Responsibly　　196
CHAPTER 7　　**209**
Overcoming Communication Barriers　　**209**
　　Handling Communication Breakdowns　　209
　　Strategies for Communicating with Vulnerable Populations　　219
　　Dealing with Language Barriers and Disabilities　　231
CHAPTER 8　　**245**
Practice Makes Perfect: Drills and Simulations 245
　　Planning and Conducting Communication Drills　　245
　　Evaluating and Improving Your Communication Plan　　255
　　Involving Community and Neighbors in Drills 265

CHAPTER 9   **277**
Advanced Communication Techniques for Preppers   **277**
    Mesh Networks and Off-Grid Internet   277
    Encrypted Communications for Privacy and Security   286
    Utilizing Morse Code and Other Non-Verbal Communication Methods   296

CHAPTER 10   **305**
Real-Life Case Studies and Lessons Learned   305
    Success Stories of Effective Emergency Communication   305
    Analyzing Failures and Learning from Mistakes   313
    Adapting Lessons to Your Personal Plan   322

CONCLUSION   **331**
    The Road to Resilient Communication: Next Steps   331

INTRODUCTION

The Importance of Emergency Communication

During emergencies and disasters, communication becomes one of the most important tools we have. Imagine you're in the middle of a big storm, and the power goes out. You can't turn on the TV to see what's happening, and your phone isn't working because the cell towers are down. This situation can be scary and confusing, especially if you don't know what's going on or how to contact your loved ones. This is where emergency communication comes in. It's all about staying connected and making sure everyone knows what to do and where to go when something unexpected happens.

Emergency communication is crucial for several reasons. First, it helps keep people safe. When disaster strikes, getting accurate and timely information can make a huge difference. Knowing whether to evacuate or stay indoors, understanding which areas are safe, and receiving updates about the situation are all pieces of information that can protect you and your family. For example, if a wildfire is approaching your neighborhood, an emergency alert can tell you when and where to evacuate for safety. Without such communication, you might not realize the danger until it's too late.

Also, emergency communication helps families and communities coordinate their actions. In a disaster, it's important for everyone to work together. Families need to make sure they can reach each other and have a plan for where to meet if they get separated. This is especially important if different family members are in different locations when the emergency happens, like at school or work. Communities too, need to be able to communicate effectively to help those who are most vulnerable, such as the elderly, people with disabilities, and children. By sharing information and resources, communities can respond more effectively and help more people.

Moreover, emergency communication is vital for information sharing. In the chaos of a disaster, rumors and false information can spread quickly, leading to panic and making the situation worse. Reliable communication helps to prevent this by providing clear, accurate information about what's happening and what people should do. For instance, during a flood, some areas might be more dangerous than others due to rapidly rising water levels. Accurate communication ensures that people receive the correct information and can take the appropriate actions to stay safe.

In addition to keeping people informed about immediate dangers, emergency communication also helps people prepare for what's coming next. Disasters often disrupt basic services like water, electricity, and transportation, sometimes for days or even weeks. Through effective communication, authorities can provide updates on when services might be restored, where to find help, and what supplies might be needed. This information is critical for helping people make decisions about whether to stay where they are or move to a safer location.

Emergency communication isn't just about official alerts from government agencies or news organizations. It's also about the everyday ways people stay in touch with one another. Friends, neighbors, and family members can play a big role in sharing information and supporting each other during emergencies. For example, neighbors might share resources like food and water, or help each other evacuate if necessary. Having a plan for how to communicate with the people around you can make a big difference in how well you cope with a disaster.

There are many different tools and methods for emergency communication, each with its strengths and limitations. Some people might use radios, which can work even when cell phones and the internet are down. Others might rely on satellite phones, which are more expensive but can be very reliable in remote areas. Text messaging and social media can also be useful, especially if you have a smartphone and internet access. Even simple things like whistles, flashlights, and hand signals can be important ways to communicate when technology fails.

One important aspect of emergency communication is having a plan in place before a disaster occurs. This means thinking ahead about how you'll communicate with your family and what you'll do if you get separated. It might involve choosing a meeting place where everyone knows to go if something happens, or setting up a phone tree where each person is responsible for calling one or two others. Practicing this plan regularly helps ensure that everyone knows what to do and can act quickly in an emergency.

Another key part of emergency communication is understanding and using different types of emergency alerts. These can include warnings sent out by government agencies, weather alerts, and notifications from local authorities. Knowing how to receive and respond to these alerts is critical. For example, many cell phones have a setting that allows them to receive emergency alerts automatically, even when other functions are turned off. This can be a lifesaver in situations where every minute counts.

It's also important to be aware of the limitations of different communication methods. In a disaster, cell phone networks might become overloaded with too many people trying to make calls at the same time, or they might stop working altogether if the infrastructure is damaged. Internet connections might be unreliable, especially if there's a power outage. Understanding these limitations can help you choose the best communication tools for different situations and make sure you have backup options in place.

In addition to technical skills, good emergency communication also requires soft skills like clear speaking, active listening, and empathy. During a crisis, people are often scared and stressed, which can make communication more challenging. Being able to stay calm, speak clearly, and listen carefully can help ensure that everyone understands what's happening and what they need to do. Empathy is also important, as it helps us understand how others might be feeling and what support they might need.

Emergency communication helps build a sense of community and resilience. When people know they can count on each other and have a plan for staying in touch, they feel more secure and prepared. This sense of preparedness can reduce fear and anxiety, making it easier to handle the stress of a disaster. It also encourages people to look out for one another, which is especially important in difficult times.

Emergency communication is a vital part of preparedness for any disaster or emergency situation. It keeps people safe by providing critical information and helps families and communities coordinate their actions to support one another. By planning ahead and knowing how to use different communication tools, we can all be better prepared to face whatever challenges come our way. Whether it's through official alerts, family communication plans, or community networks, effective communication is the key to staying connected and informed when it matters most.

CHAPTER 1

Understanding the Basics of Emergency Communication

What is Emergency Communication?

Emergency communication refers to the methods and systems we use to share information when there is a crisis or disaster. It involves getting important messages across to people quickly to help them stay safe and informed. This could include everything from warning people about a natural disaster, like a hurricane or earthquake, to telling them where to find shelter, food, or medical help after something bad has happened. Emergency communication can happen through many channels, such as radios, phones, loudspeakers, social media, and even face-to-face conversations.

The purpose of emergency communication is to protect people and help them make the right decisions during difficult times. When things go wrong, whether it's a natural disaster, a big accident, or even a man-made event like a fire, having clear and reliable communication can save lives. It ensures that people know what to do, where to go, and how to get help if they need it. Emergency communication helps reduce confusion and panic by providing accurate and timely information.

- **Why is Emergency Communication Necessary**

Emergency communication is necessary in a variety of situations, each requiring specific types of information and responses. Here are some common scenarios where emergency communication is essential:

Natural Disasters: These include hurricanes, earthquakes, floods, tornadoes, and wildfires. In such situations, emergency communication systems warn people about the danger and provide instructions on how to protect themselves. For example, during a hurricane, an emergency alert might tell people to evacuate an area before the storm hits or to take shelter if they are already in a safe place.

Public Health Emergencies: Situations like pandemics, outbreaks of contagious diseases, or chemical spills require emergency communication to inform the public about how to stay safe and healthy. This might include information on symptoms to watch for, where to get medical help, or how to avoid spreading a disease. Clear communication is vital to prevent panic and ensure that people follow health guidelines.

Technological or Industrial Accidents: These are incidents like power plant failures, chemical spills, or train derailments. In such cases, emergency communication helps people understand the risks, such as exposure to toxic substances, and provides instructions on what to do, such as staying indoors or evacuating the area.

Terrorism and Security Threats: In cases of terrorist attacks or other security threats, emergency communication helps keep people safe by providing information on what has happened, where it is happening, and how to avoid danger. It can also help in coordinating emergency response efforts and keeping the public calm and informed about what to expect next.

Community and Household Emergencies: On a smaller scale, emergencies like house fires, gas leaks, or missing children require quick and effective communication within a community or household. Here, emergency communication could involve calling emergency services, alerting neighbors, or using local networks to spread the word and coordinate a response.

- **Key Components of Emergency Communication**

To understand emergency communication fully, it's helpful to break it down into key components. These components are crucial for making sure that messages are clear, accurate, and received by the right people at the right time.

Alerting Systems: These systems are designed to catch people's attention and provide immediate warnings about an ongoing or imminent threat. This might include sirens, emergency broadcasts on radio and TV, mobile phone alerts, and even door-to-door notifications. Alerting systems are usually the first step in emergency communication and are vital for getting people to take immediate action, like evacuating or taking shelter.

Information Dissemination: After the initial alert, it's important to keep people informed about what's happening. This can include updates about the severity of the situation, safety instructions, and information about available resources like shelters and medical facilities. Information dissemination happens through various channels, such as social media, news broadcasts, and community networks, ensuring that as many people as possible have access to the information they need.

Two-Way Communication: While getting information out is important, emergency communication also involves receiving information. This can be through reports from the public about their needs or the current situation, or through communication with emergency responders and officials coordinating the response. Two-way communication helps authorities understand what's happening on the ground and make better decisions about how to respond to the emergency.

Coordination and Command: In any emergency, there are many people and organizations involved in the response. Effective emergency communication ensures that everyone is on the same page and working together. This means coordinating between different emergency services, like police, fire, and medical teams, as well as with community organizations, government agencies, and even volunteers. Coordination helps make sure resources are used effectively and responses are organized.

- **How Emergency Communication Works in Different Scenarios**

In different emergency scenarios, communication needs and methods may vary. Here's how emergency communication might work in some specific situations:

During a Hurricane: Before the storm hits, emergency communication systems might send out alerts via mobile phones, radios, and TVs, warning people about the hurricane's path and urging them to evacuate or prepare their homes. Local authorities may use social media to provide ongoing updates about the storm's progress and where people can find shelters. After the hurricane, communication efforts focus on informing people about safety hazards, such as downed power lines or flooded roads, and guiding them to resources like food, water, and medical care.

In an Earthquake: Earthquakes often strike without warning, so the focus of emergency communication is usually on the aftermath. Authorities might use all available channels, including radio, TV, social media, and text alerts, to provide information on aftershocks, areas to avoid, and where to find emergency services. Communication also involves coordinating rescue and relief efforts, ensuring that help reaches those who need it most.

During a Pandemic: In a health emergency like a pandemic, emergency communication plays a critical role in educating the public about how to prevent the spread of the disease. This might include messages about wearing masks, practicing social distancing, and getting vaccinated.

Communication is ongoing and needs to be consistent to keep people informed as the situation evolves. It also involves countering misinformation and ensuring that the public trusts the information they are receiving.

- **Importance of Accessibility in Emergency Communication**

Accessibility is a critical aspect of emergency communication. Information must reach everyone, including people with disabilities, the elderly, children, and non-English speakers. This means using multiple communication methods to ensure everyone can access important information.

For People with Disabilities: Emergency communication should include formats that are accessible to people with different types of disabilities. For example, visual alerts for those who are deaf, audio descriptions for those who are blind, and simple, clear language for those with cognitive disabilities.

For Non-English Speakers: In diverse communities, emergency communication must be multilingual. This ensures that everyone, regardless of the language they speak, receives the same critical information. Multilingual communication can be achieved through translations, using local radio stations that broadcast in different languages, and by working with community leaders who can help spread the word.

For Children and Elderly People: Messages need to be age-appropriate and considerate of the needs and abilities of different age groups. For children, this might mean using simpler language and ensuring that parents and guardians are informed and can help guide them. For elderly people, communication might involve checking in through neighbors or community organizations to make sure they understand the information and have access to resources.

Emergency communication is more than just sending out warnings; it's about ensuring everyone has the information they need to stay safe and make informed decisions during crises. By understanding what emergency communication is and how it works across different scenarios, we can better appreciate its importance and work towards improving it in our communities. Whether through alert systems, public information campaigns, or direct communication with responders, effective emergency communication is essential for keeping people safe and informed when it matters most.

Why Communication Fails During Disaster

When disasters strike, communication is crucial for ensuring people's safety and coordinating effective responses. However, many times during emergencies, communication systems fail, making it difficult for people to get the information they need. There are several reasons why communication systems break down during disasters, including power outages, network congestion, and damaged infrastructure. Understanding these challenges can help us better prepare and find ways to ensure that important messages still get through when they are most needed.

- **Power Outages**

One of the most common reasons communication fails during disasters is because of power outages. Disasters like hurricanes, earthquakes, and floods can cause widespread damage to electrical power lines and power stations, leading to blackouts that can last hours, days, or even weeks. Without power, many communication devices, such as phones, computers, and radios, simply do not work.

Impact on Communication Devices: Most communication devices rely on electricity to function. For example, cell phones need to be charged, internet routers require power, and even landline phones in modern homes often rely on electric power. When there is no electricity, these devices cannot be used to make calls, send messages, or access the internet. This makes it incredibly difficult for people to stay in touch with loved ones or receive updates on the situation.

Effect on Communication Infrastructure: Power outages also affect the infrastructure that supports communication. Cell towers, which are essential for mobile phone communication, need electricity to operate. Many cell towers have backup generators, but these generators can only provide power for a limited amount of time. Once the backup power runs out, the towers stop working, cutting off mobile phone communication in the affected area. Similarly, internet service providers rely on electricity to power their equipment and networks, so an extended power outage can disrupt internet access over a wide area.

- Network Congestion

Another major reason communication systems fail during disasters is network congestion. During an emergency, everyone tries to call, text, or go online to get information and contact loved ones. This sudden surge in usage can overwhelm the communication networks, causing them to slow down, become unreliable, or fail completely.

Overloaded Cell Networks: When too many people try to use their cell phones at the same time, the network becomes congested. Cell towers have a limited capacity for handling calls and data, and when this capacity is exceeded, calls may not go through, text messages might be delayed, and internet connections can become very slow or stop working altogether. This is particularly problematic in densely populated areas, where a large number of people might be trying to communicate simultaneously during a disaster.

Internet Slowdowns and Outages: Similar to cell networks, the internet can also become congested when too many people try to access it at once. Websites and online services can slow down or crash due to the high traffic. This is especially true for websites that provide emergency updates or news, as everyone tries to access them for the latest information. In addition, video calls and streaming services, which require a lot of data, can further strain the internet, making it difficult for people to communicate or receive important updates.

Impact on Emergency Services: Network congestion can also affect emergency services. During disasters, emergency responders rely on communication networks to coordinate their efforts and respond to people in need. If the networks are congested, it can delay response times and make it harder for emergency services to communicate with each other and the public. This can put lives at risk, especially if people are unable to call for help or receive instructions on what to do.

- **Damaged Infrastructure**

Communication systems can also fail during disasters because of damaged infrastructure. Many disasters, such as earthquakes, hurricanes, and floods, can cause significant damage to the physical infrastructure that supports communication, including cell towers, telephone lines, and internet cables.

Destruction of Cell Towers and Telephone Lines: Natural disasters can topple cell towers, snap telephone poles, and break underground cables. For example, high winds from a hurricane can knock over cell towers, while flooding can wash away telephone poles or damage underground internet cables. When this infrastructure is damaged or destroyed, the ability to make phone calls, send texts, or access the internet is greatly reduced or lost altogether.

Damage to Switching Centers and Data Centers: Switching centers and data centers are crucial parts of the communication infrastructure that manage the flow of data and calls. During a disaster, these facilities can also be damaged or lose power, disrupting communication services. For example, if an earthquake causes structural damage to a switching center, it might prevent calls from being routed properly, leading to dropped calls or no service at all.

Challenges with Repairing Infrastructure: Even after a disaster has passed, repairing damaged communication infrastructure can be challenging. Roads may be blocked, making it hard for repair crews to reach the damaged sites. In some cases, it might be too dangerous for crews to work immediately, such as after an earthquake when there is a risk of aftershocks. This means that communication services could be down for an extended period, complicating rescue efforts and making it harder for people to stay informed.

- **Additional Challenges Affecting Communication During Disasters**

Beyond power outages, network congestion, and damaged infrastructure, there are several other factors that can cause communication systems to fail during disasters.

Lack of Redundant Systems: Redundancy in communication systems means having multiple ways to communicate if one method fails. For example, if cell phone service is down, having a satellite phone or a two-way radio as a backup can still allow for communication. However, not all areas or organizations have redundant systems in place, and when the primary communication method fails, there may be no alternative available.

Limited Access to Communication Tools: Not everyone has access to the same communication tools. Some people may not own smartphones or computers, and others may live in areas without reliable internet or cell phone coverage even under normal conditions. During a disaster, these people are at a greater disadvantage because they have fewer ways to receive and share information.

Lack of Preparedness and Training: In some cases, communication failures during disasters occur because people are not prepared or trained to use alternative communication methods. For example, if someone does not know how to operate a two-way radio or interpret emergency signals, they may struggle to communicate when traditional methods fail. Proper training and preparedness can help ensure that people know what to do when communication systems are down.

- **Preparing for Communication Failures**

To address these challenges and improve communication during disasters, it is essential to prepare in advance. Here are some steps that can help:

Have Backup Communication Tools: It's a good idea to have backup communication tools that do not rely on the same infrastructure as your primary method. This could include battery-powered radios, satellite phones, or even whistles and flashlights for signaling in person.

Create a Communication Plan: Families and communities should have a communication plan that includes multiple ways to stay in touch if one method fails. This might involve setting up a meeting place where everyone knows to go if communication is lost or using a phone tree system to ensure that everyone gets the message.

Invest in Redundant Systems: Communities and organizations should invest in redundant communication systems to ensure they have multiple ways to communicate during a disaster. This might include setting up community radio stations, installing backup generators for cell towers, or maintaining a stockpile of communication equipment that can be deployed when needed.

Practice and Educate: Regular drills and education can help people learn how to use alternative communication methods and understand what to do when communication systems are down. This can help reduce panic and confusion during a real disaster and ensure that people know how to stay connected and informed.

While communication systems can and do fail during disasters for various reasons, understanding these challenges can help us better prepare and improve our chances of staying connected when it matters most. By having multiple communication methods, being prepared, and knowing how to use different tools, we can help ensure that important messages reach those who need them, even when disaster strikes.

Different Types of Communication Methods

In times of emergencies or disasters, having reliable communication methods is essential. When traditional systems like cell phones and landlines fail, alternative communication tools become vital for staying in touch with loved ones, coordinating with emergency responders, and receiving critical updates. Understanding the various communication methods available can help you choose the right tools for different situations and ensure you remain connected even when standard networks are down. Below are several communication methods commonly used during emergencies, including radios, satellite phones, and internet-based tools.

- **Radios**

Radios are one of the most reliable communication tools during emergencies. They don't rely on the same infrastructure as cell phones or landlines, which means they can still function when other systems fail. There are different types of radios used for emergency communication, each with unique features and benefits.

Two-Way Radios (Walkie-Talkies): Two-way radios, commonly known as walkie-talkies, are portable radios that allow people to communicate with each other over short distances. They are simple to use and don't require a network or internet connection, making them ideal for local communication. Walkie-talkies are especially useful in situations where people need to stay in touch within a small area, such as a neighborhood or a campsite. They operate on specific frequencies, and some models allow users to switch channels to avoid interference.

Amateur Radios (Ham Radios): Ham radios are a more advanced type of two-way radio that can communicate over much longer distances. Unlike walkie-talkies, which have a limited range, ham radios can reach across cities, countries, and even continents, depending on the equipment and atmospheric conditions. Ham radios require a license to operate, but they are invaluable during emergencies because they can connect people across great distances when other communication methods are unavailable. They are often used by amateur radio operators who volunteer their time and equipment to help during disasters.

Emergency Alert Radios: Emergency alert radios are designed to receive broadcasts from local and national emergency services. These radios are often used to provide updates on weather conditions, evacuation orders, and other critical information during a disaster. Some emergency alert radios can automatically turn on and broadcast emergency messages, even if they were turned off, ensuring that important alerts are not missed. They are typically battery-powered or hand-crankable, making them reliable in power outages.

- **Satellite Phones**

Satellite phones, or sat phones, are another crucial communication tool during emergencies. Unlike cell phones that rely on terrestrial cell towers, satellite phones connect directly to satellites orbiting the Earth. This makes them ideal for use in remote areas or during disasters when cell towers are down or overloaded.

Functionality and Coverage: Satellite phones can work anywhere on the planet, as long as they have a clear line of sight to the sky. This makes them an excellent choice for communication in remote locations where other methods might not work. They are also useful in situations where a disaster has caused widespread damage to ground-based communication infrastructure, such as earthquakes or tsunamis.

Durability and Reliability: Sat phones are designed to be more durable than regular cell phones, with many models being waterproof, dustproof, and shock-resistant. This makes them suitable for use in harsh environments where standard phones might easily get damaged. During an emergency, when conditions can be unpredictable, the durability of satellite phones can be a significant advantage.

Limitations: While satellite phones are reliable in many situations, they do have some limitations. They are generally more expensive than regular cell phones, both in terms of the initial cost and the cost of calls and messages. Additionally, satellite phones can struggle to connect indoors, in dense urban areas, or under heavy tree cover because they require a clear line of sight to the sky. Despite these limitations, satellite phones are an essential tool for emergency preparedness, especially in remote areas or regions prone to natural disasters.

- **Internet-Based Tools**

Internet-based communication tools are becoming increasingly popular for emergency communication. These tools can include social media platforms, messaging apps, and email. However, they do rely on having an internet connection, which can be a limitation if the infrastructure is damaged. Nevertheless, when available, internet-based tools offer several advantages for staying connected during emergencies.

Messaging Apps and Social Media: Platforms like WhatsApp, Facebook Messenger, Telegram and Twitter can be useful for sharing information quickly and widely. In times of crisis, these apps allow people to send text messages, images, videos, and voice messages to individuals or groups. Many emergency services and organizations also use social media to provide updates and share information with the public. Because these platforms often use data rather than voice networks, they may still work when cell networks are congested, making them a useful backup option.

Email: Email remains a reliable form of communication for sharing more detailed information. During an emergency, emails can be used to send longer messages, share documents, and coordinate with larger groups. Unlike phone calls, which require a live connection, emails can be sent and received even if the internet connection is slow or intermittent, as they will send as soon as the connection is stable.

Emergency Communication Apps: There are specific apps designed for emergency communication that provide additional features beyond standard messaging apps. For example, some apps allow users to share their location with emergency contacts, send distress signals, or access offline maps and emergency information. These apps are especially useful when planning for a disaster, as they can offer additional resources and tools to help keep people safe and informed.

- **Landline Phones**

While not as commonly used today as mobile phones, landline phones can still play a crucial role in emergency communication. Unlike cell phones, landlines are connected directly to a physical telephone network, which can make them more reliable in certain situations.

Below are the characteristics of landline phones:

Resilience During Power Outages: Traditional landline phones, especially those that are not cordless, do not rely on external power and can still work during power outages. This makes them a valuable communication tool when the electricity is out and mobile phones are unable to be charged. However, it's important to note that modern landline phones that connect through internet services will not work if the power is out and the internet is down.

Clear Communication: Landline phones typically provide clearer audio quality than mobile phones, which can be especially important in emergency situations where clear communication is necessary.

This makes landlines a good backup option for households during a disaster.

Limited Mobility: The main limitation of landline phones is that they are stationary. Unlike mobile phones and other portable communication devices, landlines can only be used in a specific location. This can be a disadvantage during an evacuation or in situations where people need to move frequently.

- **Two-Way Messaging Devices**

Two-way messaging devices, like those used for hiking and outdoor adventures, are designed to send text messages via satellite, even when there is no cell service. These devices can be a vital part of an emergency communication plan.

The following are the characteristics of Two-way messaging devices:

Satellite-Based Text Messaging: Devices like the Garmin inReach or SPOT X use satellite networks to send and receive text messages. This is particularly useful in remote areas where cell service is unreliable or nonexistent. They allow users to communicate their location and status to family, friends, or emergency services, making them an important tool for outdoor adventurers and emergency preparedness.

Emergency SOS Features: Many two-way messaging devices also have an emergency SOS button that can be used to send a distress signal to emergency responders. This feature can be life-saving in situations where immediate help is needed, and other communication methods are unavailable.

Limitations: Like satellite phones, two-way messaging devices require a clear view of the sky to connect to satellites. They also have a limited number of messages that can be sent and received each month, and sending messages can be slow compared to other communication methods. However, their ability to function in areas without cell service makes them an invaluable tool for emergency communication.

Each of these communication methods offers unique advantages and can be vital during emergencies. Radios provide reliable local and long-distance communication, especially when other networks fail. Satellite phones and two-way messaging devices ensure connectivity in remote areas and during major disasters that damage local infrastructure. Internet-based tools offer versatile communication options but depend on internet availability. Landline phones can be reliable during power outages but are limited by their stationary nature. By understanding the strengths and limitations of each method, individuals and families can better prepare for emergencies and ensure they have multiple ways to stay connected, receive updates, and call for help when needed.

CHAPTER 2

Preparing Your Communication Plan

Identifying Communication Needs for Your Family

When preparing for an emergency, one of the most important things to consider is how your family will stay in touch. Communication is key to ensuring everyone's safety, sharing important information, and coordinating actions during a disaster. To create an effective emergency communication plan, you first need to identify the specific communication needs of your family. This involves understanding the unique factors that affect how each family member will communicate during a crisis. These factors include your location, the ages of family members, any special requirements, and the types of emergencies that are most likely to occur. By carefully considering these elements, you can develop a communication strategy that keeps everyone connected and informed, no matter what happens.

- **Understanding Location-Based Needs**

Where your family lives plays a significant role in determining your communication needs. Different locations present unique challenges and opportunities for staying in touch during an emergency.

Urban vs. Rural Areas: If your family lives in an urban area, you might have access to more communication resources, like local emergency services, cell towers, and internet infrastructure. However, urban areas can also become congested during disasters, leading to network overloads or power outages that disrupt communication. In contrast, if your family is in a rural area, you may be further from emergency services, and cell coverage might be limited or unreliable. In this case, you might rely more on tools like satellite phones or ham radios, which don't depend on local infrastructure.

Proximity to Disaster-Prone Zones: Consider if your family lives in a region prone to specific types of disasters, such as hurricanes, earthquakes, floods, or wildfires. These different scenarios can affect how you communicate. For example, in areas prone to hurricanes, communication plans should account for power outages and flooded roads, which might limit travel and access to communication devices. On the other hand, in earthquake-prone regions, it's important to consider the potential for downed communication lines and damaged infrastructure.

Multiple Locations: If family members are spread across different locations, such as children in school, parents at work, or elderly relatives in another town, you need to consider how to keep everyone informed and connected. This might mean setting up different communication methods for each location or designating a central point of contact who can relay information to everyone. Understanding how to communicate across multiple locations is essential to ensure everyone knows what to do and where to go during an emergency.

- **Considering Age and Abilities**

The ages and abilities of your family members also significantly impact your communication plan. Each person might have different needs based on their understanding of emergencies, their ability to use communication devices, and any physical or cognitive limitations.

Children: Younger children might not fully understand how to use complex communication tools or might get scared during an emergency. It's important to teach them simple and clear instructions, like memorizing important phone numbers or knowing where to find a family meeting spot. For older children, you can teach them how to use more advanced communication devices, like two-way radios or apps on a smartphone. Consider creating a checklist or a communication card with key information, such as emergency contacts and steps to take during different types of emergencies.

Elderly Family Members: Older adults might have different needs based on their comfort level with technology and any physical limitations. They may prefer using landline phones or simpler devices with large buttons and clear displays. If they have hearing or vision impairments, ensure that communication devices are accessible, such as phones with louder volume settings or text-to-speech functions. It's also helpful to set up devices with pre-programmed contacts and emergency services numbers to make it easier for them to reach out when needed.

Individuals with Special Needs: If anyone in your family has special needs, such as mobility challenges, hearing impairments, or cognitive disabilities, it's crucial to account for these in your communication plan. For example, someone with a hearing impairment might rely more on text-based communication methods, such as text messaging or email, rather than phone calls. For those with mobility challenges, consider how they will access communication devices if they need to move quickly or if there are obstacles. It's also essential to ensure that all family members understand any specific procedures or signals used to communicate with those who have special needs.

- **Assessing Specific Requirements**

Every family is different, and each has unique communication needs based on various personal and practical factors. To create a comprehensive communication plan, assess the specific requirements that might affect how you communicate during an emergency.

Medical Needs: If someone in your family requires regular medication or medical equipment, consider how this will affect your communication plan. You may need to ensure that communication devices are easily accessible and that emergency contacts include healthcare providers or caregivers. Additionally, keep a list of medical conditions and requirements readily available, so you can quickly share this information with emergency responders if needed.

Pet and Animal Considerations: Don't forget to include pets and service animals in your communication plan. If you have pets, consider how you will communicate their needs to others in the family or emergency responders. For example, you might create a checklist of pet supplies and emergency contacts for veterinarians. If someone in your family relies on a service animal, ensure that all family members understand how to communicate any specific needs or instructions related to the animal's care during an emergency.

Backup Power and Charging: One often overlooked requirement is the need for backup power and charging options for communication devices. Make sure you have a way to keep your phones, radios, and other devices charged, especially during prolonged power outages. This could include having extra batteries, solar chargers, or hand-crank generators. It's also a good idea to have a plan for rotating device use to conserve battery life during extended emergencies.

- ## Creating a Family Communication Matrix

After assessing the various needs of your family, create a communication matrix to outline who will be responsible for communicating with whom, using which methods, and under what circumstances. This matrix serves as a clear guide for everyone in the family, so they know what to do during an emergency.

Assigning Roles and Responsibilities: Clearly define who will take on specific roles, such as contacting emergency services, updating other family members, or caring for pets. Having these roles defined in advance prevents confusion and ensures that all tasks are covered during an emergency.

Choosing Primary and Secondary Methods: Identify your primary communication method for each scenario (e.g., using a cell phone for regular updates) and a backup method (e.g., using a two-way radio if the cell phone is unavailable). Make sure everyone understands how to use both methods and knows when to switch to the backup option.

Setting Up Check-In Times: Establish regular check-in times when everyone should contact each other to confirm their status and share updates. This could be as simple as agreeing to send a quick text every hour during a storm or having a daily check-in time during a prolonged crisis. Regular check-ins help keep everyone informed and reassured, especially if separated during an emergency.

- **Regular Practice and Updates**

Once your communication plan is in place, it's essential to practice it regularly with all family members. Conduct regular drills to ensure everyone knows what to do and feels comfortable using the communication tools. This also provides an opportunity to identify any gaps or areas that need improvement.

Updating the Plan: Your family's needs and circumstances may change over time, so it's important to update your communication plan regularly. Review it every few months or after any significant changes, such as moving to a new home, adding a new family member, or experiencing a recent emergency. Keeping the plan up-to-date ensures that it remains effective and relevant.

By carefully identifying the communication needs of your family and planning accordingly, you can ensure that everyone stays connected, informed, and safe during an emergency. A well-thought-out communication plan provides peace of mind and prepares your family to handle any situation that arises.

Setting Up a Communication Tree

In times of emergency, it is vital that every family member is informed and accounted for as quickly as possible. A communication tree is a tool designed to help families stay connected during a crisis by ensuring that information is passed efficiently and accurately to everyone who needs it. Just like the branches of a tree, a communication tree spreads out from a central point, ensuring that each person in the family is reached without delay. This method helps avoid confusion and ensures that everyone knows what to do and where to go. By understanding how to set up and use a communication tree, families can enhance their preparedness for any disaster.

• What is a Communication Tree?

A communication tree is a simple, structured system that organizes how information flows within a group, such as a family, during an emergency. Imagine a tree with a trunk and many branches; the trunk represents the central point of contact, and the branches represent each family member or smaller group within the family. When an emergency occurs, the central point (usually a designated family leader) communicates the necessary information to the first set of people (the initial branches). Each of those people then communicates with another set of individuals, continuing the process until everyone in the family has received the message. This method ensures that information is shared quickly and accurately, reducing the chances of misunderstandings or delays.

Benefits of a Communication Tree

A communication tree offers several key benefits during emergencies:

Speed: By organizing who contacts whom, a communication tree speeds up the process of sharing important information. This is crucial during emergencies when every second counts.

Clarity: A communication tree reduces confusion by assigning clear responsibilities for passing along information. Each person knows who they need to contact, which prevents the duplication of effort and ensures that everyone receives the same information.

Accountability: It helps keep track of who has been contacted and who still needs to be reached. This ensures that no one is forgotten or left out during a crisis.

Reduced Overwhelm: The tree structure means that no single person is overwhelmed with the responsibility of contacting every family member. Instead, the task is broken down into manageable steps, making the communication process more efficient and less stressful for everyone involved.

- ## How to Create a Communication Tree

Creating a communication tree involves several steps to ensure that it is effective and easy to use. Here's how to set up your family's communication tree:

Identify a Central Point of Contact

The first step in creating a communication tree is to choose a central point of contact. This person is responsible for initiating the communication tree when an emergency arises. Ideally, this should be someone who is often reachable and reliable, such as a parent or another trusted adult in the family. The central contact should be someone who remains calm under pressure and is capable of quickly understanding and relaying information.

List All Family Members and Their Contact Information

Next, make a list of every family member who should be included in the communication tree. Write down their names, phone numbers, email addresses, and any other relevant contact information. If some family members live in different locations or have varying schedules, make a note of this as well. It's also helpful to include any additional emergency contacts, such as neighbors, friends, or relatives who could assist in reaching someone if direct contact isn't possible.

Organize the Family into Groups

Divide the family members into smaller groups or branches based on who would be most logical to contact next. This could be organized by proximity (such as those living in the same household or nearby), by relationship (like parents, siblings, or cousins), or by availability (those who are most likely to have access to communication devices). Each group should have a designated person responsible for contacting the others in their group. This way, the information can flow smoothly from the central contact through the various branches of the tree.

Assign Responsibilities

Assign each person in the communication tree a specific responsibility for whom they need to contact. For example, the central point of contact might be responsible for contacting three or four key family members. Each of these individuals would then contact the next person or group on their list, and so on. Make sure everyone understands their role in the communication tree and knows exactly who they are responsible for contacting.

Create a Visual Map

To make the communication tree easy to understand and use, create a visual map that outlines the structure. This can be a simple diagram that shows the central contact at the top, with lines branching out to each group and individual. Include each person's name and contact information on the map, along with a clear indication of who they need to contact. This visual aid can be a helpful reference during an emergency and ensures that everyone understands the plan.

Establish Clear Communication Methods

Decide on the primary and secondary methods of communication that will be used for the tree. For example, the primary method might be phone calls, with text messages or emails as a backup if calls can't go through. Make sure everyone in the tree is comfortable with these methods and knows how to use them. It's also important to establish a clear protocol for what to do if someone can't be reached. For instance, if a call isn't answered after three tries, the next person in line might need to take on additional contacts to ensure that information reaches everyone.

Practice Regularly

Just like any emergency plan, a communication tree needs to be practiced regularly to ensure it works smoothly in real life. Schedule regular drills with your family to practice using the communication tree. This could be done quarterly or at least twice a year, depending on your family's needs and the likelihood of emergencies in your area. Practicing helps everyone remember their responsibilities and become more comfortable with the process, which can make a big difference in an actual emergency.

Update the Tree as Needed

A communication tree should be a living document that is updated regularly. Anytime there is a change in your family, such as a new phone number, a move to a new home, or a change in family dynamics, the communication tree should be reviewed and updated accordingly. It's also a good idea to review the tree after any practice drill or real emergency to see what worked well and what could be improved.

- **Key Tips for an Effective Communication Tree**

Keep It Simple: The communication tree should be easy to understand and follow. Avoid making it overly complicated, which could lead to confusion during an emergency.

Be Prepared for Contingencies: Have backup contacts for each person in case someone is unreachable. This ensures that there is always a way to keep the communication flowing.

Ensure Everyone Has Access: Make sure every family member has a copy of the communication tree, whether digitally or printed. It's important that everyone knows where to find the tree and can access it easily when needed.

Use Code Words if Needed: In some cases, it might be helpful to use simple code words or phrases that indicate specific actions. This can help convey information quickly without needing to go into lengthy explanations, which can be particularly useful in noisy or chaotic situations.

Stay Calm and Follow the Plan: During an emergency, it's natural to feel anxious or scared. Remind everyone to stay calm and stick to the communication plan. Trusting the plan can help reduce stress and ensure that everyone remains informed and connected.

A communication tree is a vital tool for families preparing for emergencies. By setting up a clear, structured plan for how to share information quickly and efficiently, you can ensure that every family member is informed and accounted for during a disaster. Remember to keep the tree simple, practice regularly, and update it as needed to keep it effective. With a well-organized communication tree in place, your family will be better prepared to stay connected and safe, no matter what challenges come your way.

Developing a Family Emergency Communication Plan

A family emergency communication plan is essential for ensuring that everyone stays safe and informed during a crisis. Emergencies can strike without warning, whether they are natural disasters like earthquakes and floods, or man-made incidents like fires or power outages. When such events occur, it's crucial that family members know how to reach one another, where to go, and what to do. Creating a detailed and well-organized communication plan can help reduce panic and confusion, allowing everyone to respond quickly and effectively. Below is a step-by-step guide to developing a comprehensive family emergency communication plan, tailored to your family's specific needs.

- **Step 1: Identify Key Contacts**

The first step in creating a family emergency communication plan is to identify key contacts.

These are the people who will play an important role in relaying information and helping to coordinate the family's response during an emergency. Key contacts typically include:

Primary Family Contacts: This includes the parents or guardians and any adult family members who will take the lead in managing the family's response. These contacts should be easily reachable and knowledgeable about the emergency plan.

Extended Family or Close Friends: Include the names and contact information of relatives or close friends who do not live in the same household but are trusted to assist in an emergency. These people can serve as backup contacts if immediate family members are unreachable.

Out-of-Area Contacts: Designate at least one person who lives outside your immediate area as a contact. In some situations, local communication channels may be disrupted, but long-distance communication may still be possible. An out-of-area contact can serve as a central point of communication for everyone in the family.

Emergency Services: Keep a list of local emergency services such as police, fire department, hospitals, and other relevant agencies. These contacts should be easily accessible and include both phone numbers and addresses.

Make sure that everyone in the family knows who these key contacts are and has their contact information readily available. It's also a good idea to distribute a printed list of these contacts to each family member, as well as save them on mobile devices.

- **Step 2: Determine Communication Channels**

Next, decide on the communication channels your family will use during an emergency. Different situations may call for different methods of communication, so it's important to be familiar with all the options available to you. Common communication channels include:

Cell Phones: Mobile phones are often the first line of communication during an emergency. Ensure that all family members have working cell phones and that they keep them charged. It's also wise to invest in portable chargers or power banks, especially if you live in an area prone to power outages.

Text Messaging: In many cases, text messages can get through even when voice calls cannot, particularly if networks are congested. Encourage family members to use text messaging as a backup if they cannot make voice calls.

Landline Phones: Although less common today, landline phones can still be valuable in an emergency, particularly if mobile networks are down. If you have a landline, ensure that everyone in the family knows how to use it and where to find it.

Radios: Two-way radios (walkie-talkies) or ham radios can be critical during emergencies when other communication methods fail. If your family has access to these, make sure everyone knows how to operate them and understands the appropriate frequencies to use.

Social Media and Apps: Online platforms and emergency communication apps can be useful for sending updates and checking in with others. Familiarize your family with relevant apps, such as those provided by local authorities or emergency services, and ensure they are installed on everyone's devices.

Choose primary and secondary communication channels for your family and make sure everyone understands how to use them. It's also important to practice using these channels regularly, so everyone feels confident in their ability to communicate during a crisis.

- **Step 3: Establish Emergency Meeting Points**

In the event that family members are separated during an emergency, it's important to have predetermined meeting points where everyone can reunite. Establishing these locations in advance can save valuable time and reduce stress during a crisis. Consider the following types of meeting points:

Primary Meeting Point (Home): The first meeting point should be your home or a safe location nearby. This is where everyone should try to gather if it's safe to do so. Make sure that everyone knows how to get there and has multiple routes they can take in case certain roads or paths are blocked.

Secondary Meeting Point (Neighborhood): In case it's not safe to return home, choose a secondary meeting point in your neighborhood. This could be a nearby park, community center, or another familiar location. Ensure that this spot is easily accessible and that everyone knows how to reach it.

Out-of-Area Meeting Point: If your entire neighborhood or town is affected, it's important to have an out-of-area meeting point where the family can gather. This could be a relative's house in a nearby town or another safe location outside the immediate area. Make sure that everyone knows the address and how to get there.

Discuss these meeting points with your family and practice reaching them from different locations. It's also helpful to have a map with these locations marked and to review the routes regularly.

- **Step 4: Create an Information Distribution Plan**

An effective family emergency communication plan should also include a strategy for distributing critical information. This ensures that everyone is informed and knows what to do, even if direct communication isn't possible. Here's how to set up an information distribution plan:

Central Information Hub: Designate one person (usually the primary family contact) as the central hub for information. This person will be responsible for gathering updates from news sources, local authorities, and other contacts, and then distributing this information to the rest of the family.

Communication Tree: Create a communication tree, where each person is responsible for contacting one or more other family members. This tree structure ensures that information is passed quickly and accurately without overwhelming any one person.

Pre-Written Messages: Prepare pre-written messages for different scenarios, such as "I'm safe," "I need help," or "Meet at the secondary meeting point." These messages can be used to quickly convey important information without confusion.

Regular Check-Ins: Establish a schedule for regular check-ins, even when no emergency is currently happening. This keeps everyone in the habit of staying in touch and ensures that communication lines remain open.

- **Step 5: Practice and Review the Plan**

A communication plan is only effective if everyone knows how to use it. Regular practice and review are essential for ensuring that your family can respond quickly and efficiently during an emergency. Here's how to keep the plan fresh in everyone's mind:

Conduct Drills: Schedule regular emergency drills where your family practices using the communication plan. Simulate different scenarios, such as a power outage or a natural disaster, and have everyone follow the plan to ensure it works smoothly.

Update the Plan Regularly: Review the plan at least once a year or whenever there's a significant change in your family's situation (such as a move or a new family member). Make any necessary updates to contact information, communication channels, or meeting points.

Gather Feedback: After each drill or actual emergency, gather feedback from family members about what worked well and what could be improved. Use this feedback to refine the plan and make it even more effective.

Stay Informed: Keep up to date with new technologies, apps, and local emergency procedures that could improve your communication plan. Incorporate any relevant changes into your plan as needed.

Developing a family emergency communication plan is a crucial step in ensuring the safety and well-being of your loved ones during a crisis. By identifying key contacts, choosing reliable communication channels, establishing meeting points, and regularly practicing the plan, you can help your family stay connected and informed when it matters most. Remember, the goal is to create a plan that is easy to understand and follow, giving everyone the confidence to act quickly and effectively in an emergency.

CHAPTER 3

Tools and Technologies for Emergency Communication

Handheld Radios

Handheld radios are essential tools for emergency communication, especially when other methods like cell phones and internet-based communication might fail. They are portable, reliable, and work independently of any network infrastructure. Understanding the different types of handheld radios, including CB, Ham, and FRS/GMRS radios, will help you choose the right tool for your needs. Each type of radio has its own features, range, and licensing requirements, so it's important to know how they work and when to use them.

- **Citizens Band (CB) Radios**

CB radios are one of the most popular types of handheld radios for emergency communication. They operate on 40 shared channels within the 27 MHz frequency band and are commonly used by truckers, hobbyists, and emergency response teams. Here are some key features of CB radios:

Range: CB radios typically have a range of 1 to 5 miles, depending on the terrain and the power output of the radio. The range can be extended with the use of external antennas or repeaters, but they are limited by the relatively low power (up to 4 watts) they can legally use.

No License Required: One of the main advantages of CB radios is that they do not require a license to operate. This makes them accessible to anyone who wants a simple, straightforward way to communicate during emergencies.

Best for Short-Range Communication: Due to their limited range, CB radios are best suited for short-range communication, such as communicating with family members or neighbors within a few miles. They are particularly useful in rural areas where other forms of communication might not be available.

Channels and Usage: CB radios have 40 channels, and channel 9 is traditionally reserved for emergency communications, while channel 19 is commonly used by truckers for general communication. Knowing which channels to use can help you effectively communicate during emergencies.

CB radios are a good choice for those who need a basic, easy-to-use communication tool without the need for licensing. They are most effective in flat, open areas where the range can be maximized.

- **Ham Radios (Amateur Radios)**

Ham radios, or amateur radios, are highly versatile communication tools that can operate on a wide range of frequencies and power levels. Unlike CB radios, ham radios require a license to operate, but they offer many advantages for emergency communication:

Range: Ham radios have a much greater range than CB radios, often reaching hundreds or even thousands of miles, depending on the power level and frequency band used. This makes them ideal for long-distance communication, such as coordinating with emergency responders or staying in touch with family members who are far away.

Licensing Requirements: To operate a ham radio, you need to pass an exam and obtain a license from the Federal Communications Commission (FCC) in the United States or the relevant authority in your country. There are different levels of licenses, each granting access to different frequency bands and power levels. The most common license for beginners is the Technician class, which allows access to VHF and UHF bands.

Best for Versatile and Long-Range Communication: Ham radios are best suited for those who need a versatile communication tool that can handle both short-range and long-range communication. They are especially useful in disaster situations where traditional communication infrastructure is damaged or overloaded.

Emergency Networks and Repeaters: Ham radio operators often participate in emergency networks and use repeaters to extend their range. Repeaters are stations that receive a signal and retransmit it at a higher power, allowing communication over much greater distances. Many communities have local ham radio clubs that provide training and support for new operators.

Ham radios are a powerful tool for emergency communication, but they require a commitment to learning and practice. If you are serious about emergency preparedness and want a communication tool that can handle any situation, getting a ham radio license is a valuable investment.

- **Family Radio Service (FRS) and General Mobile Radio Service (GMRS) Radios**

FRS and GMRS radios are handheld radios that operate on similar frequencies and are often sold as a combined unit. They are popular for personal and family use because they are easy to operate and provide reliable communication over short to medium distances.

Range: FRS radios typically have a range of 0.5 to 2 miles, while GMRS radios can reach up to 5 miles or more, depending on the power level and terrain. GMRS radios can use higher power levels (up to 50 watts with an external antenna), which allows for greater range than FRS radios.

Licensing Requirements: FRS radios do not require a license to operate, making them a convenient option for families and small groups. GMRS radios, on the other hand, require a license from the FCC in the United States. The GMRS license covers an entire family and does not require a test, making it easier to obtain than a ham radio license.

Best for Family and Local Communication: FRS and GMRS radios are best suited for family use and local communication. They are ideal for keeping in touch with family members during outdoor activities, camping trips, or emergencies within a neighborhood or community.

Channels and Privacy Codes: Both FRS and GMRS radios operate on shared channels within the UHF frequency band. Many models come with privacy codes, which help reduce interference from other users on the same channel. However, it's important to note that privacy codes do not provide true privacy; they simply filter out signals from other users on the same frequency.

FRS and GMRS radios are a great option for families who want a simple, effective way to communicate during emergencies without the need for extensive training or licensing. They are easy to use and widely available, making them a popular choice for preppers and outdoor enthusiasts.

- **Comparing the Radios**

When choosing a handheld radio for emergency communication, it's important to consider the specific needs of your family and the types of emergencies you are preparing for. Here's a quick comparison of the different types of radios:

CB Radios: Best for short-range communication in rural areas, no license required, limited range and power.

Ham Radios: Best for versatile and long-range communication, requires a license, offers access to a wide range of frequencies and power levels, suitable for serious emergency preparedness.

Best for family and local communication, FRS requires no license, GMRS requires a simple license, offers short to medium range with higher power for GMRS.

Each type of radio has its own strengths and weaknesses, and the best choice will depend on your specific situation. For many families, having a combination of these radios can provide the flexibility and redundancy needed to handle a wide range of emergency scenarios.

- **Best Practices for Using Handheld Radios**

To ensure that your handheld radios are effective during emergencies, it's important to follow some best practices:

Regular Practice: Familiarize yourself and your family with how to operate the radios, including changing channels, adjusting volume, and using privacy codes. Regular practice will help everyone feel confident in using the radios when needed.

Battery Management: Keep extra batteries or rechargeable battery packs on hand, and make sure your radios are fully charged. Consider investing in a solar charger or hand-crank generator to keep your radios powered during extended emergencies.

Antenna Upgrades: For CB and ham radios, consider upgrading to a higher-quality antenna to improve range and signal clarity. A good antenna can make a significant difference in the performance of your radio.

Communication Protocols: Establish clear communication protocols with your family, such as which channels to use, when to check in, and what codes or phrases to use for specific situations. This will help ensure that everyone stays on the same page during an emergency.

Stay Informed: Join local radio clubs or online communities to stay informed about the latest developments in emergency communication and radio technology. Networking with other radio enthusiasts can provide valuable insights and support.

By understanding the different types of handheld radios and how to use them effectively, you can ensure that your family is prepared to communicate during any emergency. Whether you choose CB, ham, or FRS/GMRS radios, having a reliable communication tool is a key component of any emergency preparedness plan.

Satellite Phones: Pros and Cons

Satellite phones, or satphones, are unique communication tools that use satellites orbiting the Earth to transmit signals. Unlike traditional cell phones that rely on local cell towers, satellite phones connect directly to satellites, making them an essential option for communication during emergencies, especially in remote areas where other communication methods might not work. However, like all technologies, satellite phones have their own set of advantages and disadvantages that should be considered when deciding if they are the right choice for your emergency communication plan.

- **Pros of Satellite Phones**

Satellite phones offer several distinct advantages, particularly in situations where other communication methods fail. Here are some key benefits:

Global Coverage: One of the biggest advantages of satellite phones is their ability to provide global coverage. Because they communicate directly with satellites orbiting the Earth, satellite phones can work almost anywhere, including in remote areas, mountains, deserts, and even at sea. This makes them ideal for emergency situations where traditional cell phone networks may not be available.

Independence from Local Infrastructure: Satellite phones do not rely on local cell towers or ground-based infrastructure. This independence is crucial during natural disasters, such as earthquakes, hurricanes, or floods, where local communication infrastructure may be damaged or destroyed. In these situations, satellite phones can provide a reliable means of communication when other methods fail.

Reliable Communication in Remote Areas: For people who live in or frequently travel to remote areas where there is little or no cell coverage, satellite phones are an invaluable tool. They allow users to stay connected with emergency services, family, and friends, no matter how isolated their location might be. This makes satellite phones especially popular among adventurers, explorers, sailors, and researchers who operate in remote regions.

Emergency Features: Many satellite phones come with built-in emergency features such as GPS tracking, emergency SOS buttons, and the ability to send distress signals to rescue services. These features can be lifesaving in situations where immediate help is needed and conventional communication methods are unavailable.

Durability: Satellite phones are typically built to be rugged and durable, designed to withstand harsh conditions such as extreme temperatures, rain, dust, and physical impact. This durability makes them suitable for use in challenging environments, where other devices might fail.

These advantages make satellite phones a reliable option for emergency communication, especially in scenarios where other devices might not function properly. However, it's also important to understand their limitations to make an informed decision.

- **Cons of Satellite Phones**

While satellite phones offer several benefits, they also have some drawbacks that need to be considered:

High Cost: One of the primary disadvantages of satellite phones is their cost. The price of purchasing a satellite phone can be quite high compared to regular cell phones. Additionally, the cost of using a satellite phone can also be expensive, with high per-minute rates for calls and fees for text messages or data usage. This makes satellite phones less accessible for some families and individuals who might not have the budget for such an investment.

Signal Interference and Latency: Satellite phones rely on a clear line of sight to the sky to maintain a strong connection with satellites. This means that their signals can be blocked or interfered with by tall buildings, dense foliage, mountains, or heavy cloud cover. Furthermore, there can be a slight delay or latency in communication due to the long distance the signals must travel to reach satellites and then back to Earth. This can make conversations less smooth compared to traditional cell phone calls.

Limited Battery Life: The power consumption of satellite phones is typically higher than that of regular cell phones due to the energy required to transmit signals to satellites. This can result in a shorter battery life, especially when the phone is used frequently or continuously searching for a satellite signal. During extended emergencies, it might be challenging to keep the phone charged, especially if there is no access to reliable power sources.

Not Ideal for Indoor Use: Satellite phones generally do not work well indoors or in enclosed spaces where the signal to the satellite may be obstructed. This limitation can be problematic in emergencies where individuals need to communicate from within buildings or shelters. To use a satellite phone effectively, you often need to be outside with a clear view of the sky, which may not always be possible or safe during certain types of emergencies.

Complexity of Use: Unlike regular cell phones, which are straightforward and user-friendly, satellite phones can be more complex to operate. Users may need to learn specific steps to connect to satellites, manage their devices, and understand the limitations of the technology. This learning curve can be a barrier, especially in high-stress emergency situations where ease of use is critical.

Regulatory Restrictions: In some countries, the use of satellite phones is restricted or requires special permits. This can limit their availability and use in certain regions. It's important to check the regulations in your area or any area you plan to travel to ensure that you can legally use a satellite phone.

- **Weighing the Pros and Cons**

When deciding whether to include a satellite phone in your emergency communication plan, it's important to weigh these pros and cons against your specific needs and circumstances. Here are some factors to consider:

Location: If you live in or frequently travel to remote areas where traditional communication networks are unreliable or nonexistent, a satellite phone could be an essential tool for staying connected during emergencies.

Budget: Consider your budget and whether you can afford the upfront cost and ongoing usage fees associated with satellite phones. If cost is a major concern, you might need to explore other communication options that fit within your budget.

Frequency of Use: Think about how often you would need to use the satellite phone. If you only require it for occasional trips or rare emergencies, renting a satellite phone might be a more cost-effective option than purchasing one outright.

Type of Emergencies: Consider the types of emergencies you are most likely to face. For natural disasters that might damage local communication infrastructure, a satellite phone could be invaluable. However, if you are primarily preparing for urban emergencies where other communication tools might suffice, the high cost of a satellite phone might not be justified.

Accessibility and Training: Ensure that all potential users of the satellite phone are comfortable with its operation and understand how to use it effectively in an emergency. This might involve training sessions or regular practice to build familiarity and confidence.

- **Making the Decision**

Ultimately, the decision to invest in a satellite phone should be based on a careful assessment of your specific needs, risks, and resources. Satellite phones can provide a vital lifeline in situations where other communication methods fail, but they are not without their limitations. By understanding both the advantages and disadvantages, you can make an informed choice that best supports your emergency preparedness goals.

For many preppers, a satellite phone is an important part of a comprehensive emergency communication plan, offering a reliable backup option when all else fails. Whether used as a primary communication tool in remote areas or a secondary option to complement other devices, satellite phones can provide peace of mind and security when it matters most.

Mobile Apps and Online Platforms for Emergency Use

In today's digital age, mobile apps and online platforms have become essential tools for emergency communication. These tools allow people to stay connected, share information, and receive real-time updates during emergencies. They can be particularly useful when traditional communication methods, such as phone lines and radios are unavailable or unreliable. However, like all technologies, mobile apps and online platforms have their features and limitations that should be carefully considered when planning for emergencies.

- **Features of Mobile Apps and Online Platforms for Emergencies**

Mobile apps and online platforms designed for emergency use come with a variety of features that can help individuals and families communicate more effectively during crises. Here are some key features:

Real-Time Alerts and Notifications: Many emergency apps provide real-time alerts and notifications about severe weather, natural disasters, and other emergencies. These alerts are typically sent directly to the user's phone, ensuring that they receive critical information as quickly as possible. For example, apps like FEMA and the Red Cross Emergency app offer customizable alerts for different types of emergencies, allowing users to stay informed about potential dangers in their area.

Location Sharing: One of the most valuable features of emergency communication apps is the ability to share your location with others. This feature can be particularly helpful if someone is lost or needs to be rescued. Apps like Life360 and Google Maps allow users to share their real-time location with family and friends, making it easier for loved ones to track each other's whereabouts during an emergency. Some apps also include an SOS button that sends an immediate alert to emergency contacts with the user's location.

Emergency Contact Lists: Emergency apps often allow users to create and store a list of emergency contacts. This can be helpful for quickly notifying loved ones or emergency services in a crisis. Some apps, like ICE (In Case of Emergency), even provide medical information and emergency contact details on the phone's lock screen, allowing first responders to access critical information quickly.

Offline Capabilities: During emergencies, internet connectivity may be disrupted. To address this, some apps offer offline capabilities, such as offline maps and stored emergency plans, that users can access without an internet connection. Apps like Maps.me and OsmAnd provide downloadable maps that work offline, ensuring users can still navigate and find their way even when there is no internet access.

Communication Channels: Many apps and platforms provide multiple communication channels, including text, voice, and video calls, to ensure users can stay in touch with others during an emergency. Apps like WhatsApp and Signal allow users to send messages and make calls using an internet connection, bypassing the need for traditional phone lines that might be down during a disaster.

These features can significantly enhance communication and coordination during emergencies, providing users with the tools they need to stay safe and informed. However, it is important to understand the limitations of these apps and platforms to make the most of them in a crisis.

- **Limitations of Mobile Apps and Online Platforms for Emergencies**

While mobile apps and online platforms offer many advantages for emergency communication, they also have limitations that should be considered:

Dependence on Internet Connectivity: The primary limitation of most emergency apps and online platforms is their reliance on internet connectivity. In many emergencies, such as earthquakes, hurricanes, or widespread power outages, internet service may be disrupted or unavailable. Without an internet connection, these apps and platforms may not function properly, limiting their effectiveness. This is why it is crucial to have backup communication methods, such as radios or satellite phones, that do not rely on the internet.

Battery Life Concerns: Using mobile apps and platforms for extended periods can drain a device's battery quickly, especially when using features like GPS tracking or video calls. During a prolonged emergency, conserving battery life becomes essential, and relying solely on apps that consume a lot of power may not be practical. It is important to have portable chargers or power banks on hand to keep devices charged when regular power sources are unavailable.

Data Privacy and Security Risks: Some emergency apps and online platforms collect and store user data, including location information and personal details. This can pose privacy and security risks if the data is not adequately protected. Users should be cautious about sharing sensitive information and choose apps with strong security measures, such as end-to-end encryption. It is also important to review the app's privacy policy to understand how data is used and shared.

Learning Curve and Ease of Use: In a high-stress emergency situation, simplicity and ease of use are crucial. Some apps may have a steep learning curve or require multiple steps to access critical features, which can be challenging for users who are not tech-savvy or who are panicked. Choosing apps that are intuitive and easy to navigate is important to ensure that all family members, including children and elderly individuals, can use them effectively during an emergency.

Platform Compatibility: Not all apps and platforms are compatible with all devices. Some apps may only be available for specific operating systems, such as iOS or Android, or may not function well on older devices. It is essential to check the compatibility of the apps you choose and ensure that all family members have access to the necessary devices and software.

Over-Reliance on Technology: While technology can greatly enhance emergency communication, it is important not to become overly reliant on it. Apps and online platforms can fail due to technical issues, software bugs, or hardware malfunctions. Having a comprehensive emergency communication plan that includes multiple methods of communication, such as phone calls, text messages, radios, and face-to-face meetings, is essential to ensure reliable communication in any situation.

- **Recommended Mobile Apps and Online Platforms for Emergencies**

Based on their features and usability, here are some recommended mobile apps and online platforms for emergency communication:

FEMA App: Provides real-time alerts and information about disasters, including tips on how to stay safe. It also includes a customizable emergency kit checklist and a map with open shelters.

Life360: Allows users to share their location with family members and receive alerts when someone arrives at or leaves a designated location. It also includes an SOS feature for emergencies.

Red Cross Emergency App: Offers real-time alerts for various types of emergencies, including severe weather and natural disasters. It also provides step-by-step guides on what to do during different emergencies.

WhatsApp: A popular messaging app that allows users to send text messages, voice messages, and make voice and video calls using an internet connection. It is widely used and has a simple, user-friendly interface.

Signal: A secure messaging app that provides encrypted text, voice, and video communication. It is a good choice for users concerned about privacy and security during emergencies.

Maps.me: Offers offline maps that can be downloaded in advance and used without an internet connection. This is especially useful for navigating in areas where internet service is unavailable.

Zello: A push-to-talk app that works like a walkie-talkie, allowing users to communicate with others over an internet connection. It is useful for coordinating with groups during emergencies.

- **Making the Most of Mobile Apps and Online Platforms**

To maximize the effectiveness of mobile apps and online platforms during emergencies, consider the following tips:

Download and Test Apps in Advance: Before an emergency occurs, download the necessary apps and familiarize yourself with their features. Practice using them with family members to ensure everyone knows how to operate them.

Keep Devices Charged: Regularly charge your devices and keep portable chargers or power banks available. This will help ensure that your devices remain operational during a prolonged emergency.

Update Apps Regularly: Keep your apps updated to the latest version to ensure they have the most recent features and security enhancements. This is important for maintaining the functionality and security of the apps during emergencies.

Combine Apps with Other Communication Methods: While apps can be incredibly useful, they should be part of a larger communication plan that includes other methods, such as radios, satellite phones, and in-person communication.

By understanding both the features and limitations of mobile apps and online platforms for emergency communication, you can choose the tools that best fit your needs and ensure you are prepared for any situation.

CHAPTER 4

Setting Up a Home Communication Hub

Choosing the Right Equipment for Your Hub

Creating a home communication hub is a crucial step in preparing for emergencies. A communication hub serves as the central point in your home where all communication devices and tools are set up. This hub ensures that you can stay in touch with family members, neighbors, and emergency services even when regular communication channels are down. To build an effective home communication hub, you need to carefully select the right equipment. This involves choosing the best radios, antennas, power sources, and additional tools to ensure you have reliable communication capabilities during a disaster.

- **Radios: The Heart of Your Communication Hub**

Radios are the most vital component of any home communication hub. They provide a dependable way to communicate when cell phone networks and the internet are unavailable. Here are the main types of radios you might consider for your hub:

Handheld Radios (Two-Way Radios): These are small, portable devices that allow two-way communication. They are also known as walkie-talkies and are ideal for short-distance communication within a few miles. Handheld radios are useful for keeping in touch with family members who are nearby, such as in a different part of the house or out in the yard. They are battery-operated and often have rechargeable batteries, making them easy to use in various situations. Some common types of handheld radios include FRS (Family Radio Service) and GMRS (General Mobile Radio Service) radios. FRS radios do not require a license to operate, but GMRS radios do, especially if you want to use the higher power channels for extended range.

CB Radios (Citizens Band Radios): CB radios are popular among truckers and hobbyists, offering 40 channels for local communication within a range of about 5-20 miles, depending on terrain and antenna quality. CB radios are easy to use, relatively inexpensive, and do not require a license, making them a good option for emergency communication. They can be installed in your home or vehicle and are excellent for communicating with local community members during a disaster.

Ham Radios (Amateur Radios): Ham radios are a more advanced option for emergency communication. They provide a much longer range than CB or handheld radios, allowing communication with people hundreds or even thousands of miles away. Ham radios can operate on various frequencies and bands, making them highly versatile and suitable for different situations.

However, operating a ham radio requires a license, as users must pass an exam to demonstrate their understanding of radio operation and safety. Despite the need for a license, ham radios are one of the best choices for serious preppers due to their range, versatility, and ability to connect with a vast network of other ham operators.

When choosing radios for your communication hub, consider the range you need, whether you want the option to communicate with people outside your local area, and whether you are willing to obtain a license to operate certain types of radios. A combination of different radio types can provide flexibility and redundancy, ensuring you have multiple ways to communicate during an emergency.

- **Antennas: Enhancing Your Signal**

An antenna is a critical component that determines how well your radio can send and receive signals. The right antenna can significantly increase the range and clarity of your communications. Here are some key considerations when selecting antennas for your communication hub:

Types of Antennas: There are several types of antennas, including whip antennas, dipole antennas, and directional antennas. Whip antennas are the most common and are often used with handheld radios. They are flexible, easy to install, and provide a reasonable range for local communication. Dipole antennas are longer and need to be mounted, but they offer better range and signal quality. Directional antennas, such as Yagi antennas, focus the signal in a specific direction, increasing the range and clarity for that direction. These are particularly useful if you need to communicate with a specific location, such as a distant town or a relative's house.

Antenna Placement: The placement of your antenna is crucial for maximizing signal strength and range. Ideally, antennas should be placed as high as possible, such as on the roof of your house or on a tall pole. Higher placement reduces obstructions like buildings and trees that can block or weaken signals. It's also important to consider the surrounding environment; placing an antenna away from metal objects and other electronic devices can help reduce interference and improve signal clarity.

Antenna Compatibility: Not all antennas are compatible with all radios, so it's important to choose an antenna that works with your specific equipment. Check the frequency range and connector type of your radios and match them with the appropriate antenna. Many radios come with their own antennas, but upgrading to a more powerful antenna can significantly improve performance, especially for ham radios where long-distance communication is desired.

Having the right antennas for your radios can greatly enhance your communication hub's effectiveness, allowing you to maintain clear and reliable communication even in challenging conditions.

- **Power Sources: Keeping Your Hub Operational**

During an emergency, maintaining power for your communication devices is essential. Power outages are common during disasters, so it's important to have reliable power sources for your communication hub. Here are some options to consider:

Battery Backup: Most radios, especially handheld models, operate on batteries. Keeping a stockpile of fresh batteries on hand is a simple way to ensure your radios stay operational. For radios with rechargeable batteries, consider having a few spare battery packs that are kept fully charged and ready to use. Battery backup is the simplest and most portable power option, but it requires regular checks and replacement of expired batteries.

Solar Power: Solar panels can provide a renewable power source for your communication hub. Small, portable solar chargers are available for handheld radios and other small devices, while larger solar panels can power base station radios and charge battery packs. Solar power is particularly useful because it can provide energy during extended power outages, but it relies on sunlight, so having a secondary power option is wise for cloudy days or nighttime use.

Generators: Portable generators offer a powerful and reliable way to keep your communication hub running during long-term power outages. Generators can power multiple devices, including radios, lights, and other essential equipment. When choosing a generator, consider the fuel type (gasoline, propane, or diesel), fuel availability, and the generator's wattage capacity to ensure it meets your needs. Generators do require regular maintenance and a supply of fuel, which should be safely stored and rotated to keep fresh.

Uninterruptible Power Supply (UPS): A UPS system provides a temporary power source during short outages, allowing you to keep your devices running without interruption. UPS units contain batteries that provide power when the main electricity supply fails. They are particularly useful for protecting sensitive equipment like computers and radios from power surges and can keep your communication hub operational for a limited time until a more permanent power solution, like a generator, can be activated.

By choosing the right power sources and keeping them well-maintained, you can ensure that your communication hub remains functional during any emergency, providing a lifeline for you and your family.

- **Additional Tools for a Comprehensive Hub**

Beyond radios, antennas, and power sources, several additional tools can enhance the effectiveness of your home communication hub:

Signal Amplifiers: Signal amplifiers, or boosters, increase the strength of your radio signals, extending the range and improving clarity. They are particularly useful in areas with poor signal strength or when using radios with limited power output. Amplifiers can be used with various types of radios, including handheld, CB, and ham radios.

Backup Communication Devices: Having multiple communication devices in your hub ensures redundancy and flexibility. In addition to radios, consider having a satellite phone as a backup option. Satellite phones do not rely on local infrastructure and can provide reliable communication when other methods fail. Similarly, keeping a few extra handheld radios and batteries can ensure you always have a working device available.

Protective Cases and Storage: Protecting your equipment from damage is crucial, especially in emergencies. Sturdy, waterproof cases can protect radios, antennas, and other equipment from physical damage and environmental factors like rain and dust. Proper storage also helps organize your equipment, ensuring everything is easy to access when needed.

Emergency Information Resources: Keeping a collection of emergency resources, such as local emergency frequencies, contact lists, and operating manuals for your equipment, can be invaluable. Laminate important documents or store them in waterproof containers to protect them from water damage.

By carefully selecting and maintaining the right equipment for your home communication hub, you can ensure that you and your family are prepared to stay connected and informed during any emergency. Having a well-equipped hub means you can communicate effectively, coordinate with others, and access critical information when it matters most, enhancing your overall preparedness and safety.

Powering Your Communication Devices

In times of disaster, having a reliable communication plan is essential, and keeping your communication devices powered is a critical part of that plan. Whether you are using radios, satellite phones, or other electronic devices, each requires a steady power source to function properly. Disasters often lead to power outages, so it's important to have multiple backup power options to ensure your devices remain operational. Understanding the different power options: such as solar energy, batteries, and generators, can help you choose the best solution for your needs. Each method has its own advantages and limitations, and knowing how to use them effectively can make a big difference in an emergency situation.

- **Batteries: A Simple and Portable Power Source**

Batteries are one of the most straightforward and portable options for powering communication devices. They are widely available, easy to use, and come in different types to suit various devices. Here are some key points to consider when using batteries:

Types of Batteries: There are several types of batteries, including disposable alkaline batteries and rechargeable batteries like nickel-metal hydride (NiMH) and lithium-ion. Disposable batteries are convenient because they can be stored for a long time and used immediately. However, they are not reusable, which means you need to have a large supply on hand. Rechargeable batteries, on the other hand, can be used multiple times and are more cost-effective in the long run. They require a charger, but this can be a worthwhile investment if you have several devices that need regular power.

Storage and Shelf Life: Proper storage is crucial for maintaining the shelf life of batteries. Batteries should be kept in a cool, dry place and checked regularly to ensure they haven't leaked or corroded. Many batteries, especially disposable ones, have a long shelf life of up to 10 years, but it's important to check the expiration dates and rotate them periodically to ensure they are always ready for use.

Advantages of Batteries: Batteries are compact and portable, making them ideal for handheld communication devices like two-way radios. They are also relatively inexpensive and easy to find in stores. In an emergency, batteries provide a quick and reliable power source, especially for short-term needs. They are easy to replace, and you can carry spare sets to ensure your devices remain powered.

Limitations of Batteries: The main limitation of batteries is that they will eventually run out of power, especially if you are using them continuously. This is particularly true for disposable batteries, which need to be replaced frequently. Rechargeable batteries need a way to be recharged, which may not always be possible during an extended power outage. Also, different devices may require different types of batteries, so you need to ensure you have the right kinds on hand.

- **Solar Power: Harnessing Renewable Energy**

Solar power is an excellent alternative for powering communication devices during a disaster, especially when traditional power sources are unavailable. Solar panels convert sunlight into electricity, providing a renewable and sustainable source of power.

How Solar Power Works: Solar panels are made up of many small cells that capture sunlight and convert it into electricity. This electricity can be used immediately or stored in batteries for later use. Solar panels come in various sizes and power capacities, from small, portable chargers that can power a phone or a radio to larger panels capable of powering a whole communication hub.

Portable Solar Chargers: For preppers, portable solar chargers are a practical option. These small devices are lightweight and can be easily carried in a backpack or emergency kit. They are capable of charging small communication devices such as handheld radios, smartphones, and satellite phones. Some models are foldable or flexible, making them easy to pack and transport. Portable solar chargers usually have USB ports for charging devices directly, and some come with built-in batteries to store extra power.

Larger Solar Panels and Systems: Larger solar panels can be installed at home to provide a more robust power solution. These systems can charge larger batteries or power multiple devices simultaneously. Installing a solar power system at home requires a more significant investment but provides a reliable power source that can sustain multiple devices over longer periods. These systems can also be integrated with battery storage to provide power even when the sun isn't shining, such as at night or during cloudy weather.

Advantages of Solar Power: The biggest advantage of solar power is that it is renewable and virtually limitless, as long as there is sunlight. Solar power is also silent and doesn't produce any emissions, making it environmentally friendly. Once you have the solar panels and necessary equipment, there are no ongoing fuel costs, which makes it a cost-effective solution over time. Additionally, solar panels are relatively low maintenance and have a long lifespan.

Limitations of Solar Power: The effectiveness of solar power depends on the weather and the availability of sunlight. On cloudy days or during storms, solar panels may not produce enough power, and they are completely ineffective at night.

Solar panels also require an initial investment and some technical knowledge for installation and setup. While portable solar chargers are great for small devices, they may not provide enough power for larger equipment.

- **Generators: Reliable Power Backup**

Generators are a reliable and powerful option for keeping communication devices and other essential equipment running during a disaster. They convert fuel into electricity and can provide power for longer periods, making them ideal for extended outages.

Types of Generators: There are several types of generators, including gasoline, propane, and diesel-powered models. Gasoline generators are the most common and are widely available. They are typically less expensive than other types, but gasoline can be hard to store safely and has a shorter shelf life. Propane generators use liquid propane, which is easier to store and has a longer shelf life, but propane canisters can be bulky. Diesel generators are known for their durability and efficiency and are often used for heavy-duty applications. They have a longer lifespan than gasoline generators but tend to be more expensive and louder.

Portable vs. Standby Generators: Portable generators are smaller and can be moved around, making them ideal for temporary use or if you need to take them with you. They are useful for powering individual devices or small home systems. Standby generators are permanently installed outside a home or building and are connected directly to the electrical system. They automatically turn on during a power outage and can provide power to the entire home, including larger communication hubs and other essential equipment. Standby generators are more expensive and require professional installation, but they offer the convenience of automatic operation.

Fuel Storage and Safety: When using a generator, it's important to store enough fuel to keep it running during an extended outage. Fuel should be stored in approved containers in a cool, well-ventilated area away from living spaces to reduce the risk of fire or carbon monoxide poisoning. It's also essential to regularly maintain the generator, including checking the oil, replacing filters, and running it periodically to ensure it's in good working condition. Generators should never be used indoors or in enclosed spaces, as they produce carbon monoxide, which can be deadly.

Advantages of Generators: Generators provide a continuous power supply as long as there is fuel available. They can power multiple devices simultaneously, making them suitable for larger communication setups or other critical equipment in your home. Generators are also reliable and capable of running for long periods, which is crucial during extended power outages. Standby generators provide automatic backup power, reducing the need for manual setup during an emergency.

Limitations of Generators: The primary limitation of generators is their dependence on fuel, which can be challenging to store in large quantities. Fuel can also be hard to obtain during a widespread disaster. Generators are noisy and produce exhaust, which can be a concern in densely populated areas or enclosed spaces. They also require regular maintenance and can be expensive to purchase and install, particularly standby models.

- **Choosing the Right Power Options for Your Needs**

When deciding how to power your communication devices during a disaster, it's essential to consider your specific needs, the types of devices you have, and the likely duration of any outages.

Short-Term Solutions: For short-term power needs, such as during a brief power outage, batteries are a simple and effective solution. They are easy to store and use, and they don't require any special equipment. Portable solar chargers can also be useful for keeping small devices charged without relying on traditional power sources.

Long-Term Solutions: For longer outages or more severe disasters, a combination of power sources is often the best approach. Solar panels provide a renewable source of energy that doesn't depend on fuel availability, while generators offer a reliable backup when sunlight is not available. Having multiple power options ensures you are prepared for various scenarios and can keep your communication devices running no matter what happens.

Redundancy and Preparedness: Redundancy is key in emergency preparedness. By having multiple power options, such as batteries, solar chargers, and a generator, you can ensure that you are always ready to keep your communication devices operational. Regularly testing and maintaining your equipment will also help ensure everything is ready to go when you need it most.

By understanding and implementing these power options, you can build a robust and reliable system to keep your communication devices running during any disaster, helping to keep you and your family safe and connected.

Securing Your Communication Hub from Cyber Threats

In the digital age, securing your communication hub from cyber threats is just as important as ensuring your devices have power. Cyber threats like hacking, malware, and unauthorized access can compromise your communication systems, making them unreliable or even dangerous during an emergency. Understanding these threats and implementing protective measures is crucial for maintaining the integrity and security of your emergency communication setup.

- **Understanding Cyber Threats to Communication Systems**

Cyber threats can come in many forms, targeting various aspects of your communication hub. Here are some common cyber threats that could affect your emergency communication systems:

Hacking: This occurs when someone tries to gain unauthorized access to your communication devices or network. Hackers might attempt to intercept messages, disrupt communication, or take control of devices.

Malware: Short for malicious software, malware can infect your devices and network, causing them to malfunction or allowing attackers to steal sensitive information. Malware can spread through infected files, links, or websites.

Phishing: Phishing is a tactic used by cyber attackers to trick you into providing personal information, such as passwords or other credentials.

This can be done through emails, messages, or even phone calls that seem legitimate.

Denial of Service (DoS) Attacks: In a DoS attack, the attacker overwhelms your communication network with excessive traffic, making it impossible for you to use it effectively. This can be particularly disruptive during emergencies when communication is vital.

Unauthorized Access: This threat occurs when someone gains access to your communication systems without permission, either by guessing passwords or exploiting weak security settings. Unauthorized access can lead to data breaches and compromised communication.

To protect your communication hub from these threats, you need to implement several security measures and practices.

- **Encryption: Protecting Your Data**

Encryption is a process that transforms your data into a coded format that can only be read by someone who has the correct decryption key. It is a crucial tool for securing communication devices and networks.

Why Encryption Matters: Encryption ensures that even if a cyber attacker intercepts your communication, they will not be able to understand the information without the decryption key. This keeps your messages and data private and secure, preventing unauthorized access.

Types of Encryption: There are different types of encryption, such as symmetric encryption, where the same key is used to encrypt and decrypt the data, and asymmetric encryption, which uses a pair of keys (a public key for encrypting and a private key for decrypting). Asymmetric encryption is generally more secure, as the private key is never shared.

Encrypting Communication Devices: Many modern communication devices, like smartphones and radios, offer built-in encryption features. Ensure that these features are enabled, especially when transmitting sensitive information. For radios, look for models that support encrypted channels, which make it harder for unauthorized listeners to intercept your communications.

Securing Online Communication: For communication that involves the internet, such as emails or instant messaging, use services that provide end-to-end encryption. This means that the message is encrypted on the sender's device and only decrypted on the receiver's device, ensuring that no one else can read it in transit.

- **Secure Network Practices**

Protecting your communication hub from cyber threats also involves securing the networks that your devices use to communicate.

Setting Up a Secure Wi-Fi Network: If your communication hub relies on Wi-Fi, it's crucial to secure your network to prevent unauthorized access. Start by changing the default name (SSID) of your network to something unique and avoid using easily guessed names. Always use a strong, complex password for your Wi-Fi, combining letters, numbers, and special characters.

Using Strong Encryption for Wi-Fi: When setting up your Wi-Fi network, ensure that you are using the most secure encryption protocol available, such as WPA3. Older encryption standards like WEP and WPA2 are more vulnerable to hacking.

Regularly Updating Firmware and Software: Keep all your devices, including routers and communication devices, up to date with the latest firmware and software updates. These updates often include patches for security vulnerabilities that could be exploited by hackers.

Disabling Unused Features: Many communication devices come with features that you might not need or use. Disable any unnecessary features or services that could be exploited by attackers. For example, if your router supports remote management but you don't use it, turn it off to reduce potential attack vectors.

Creating a Guest Network: If you have visitors who need to use your Wi-Fi, create a separate guest network that is isolated from your main communication hub. This prevents them from accessing your primary network and devices, reducing the risk of accidental or intentional security breaches.

- **Using Firewalls and Antivirus Software**

Firewalls and antivirus software are critical components of a secure communication hub.

Understanding Firewalls: A firewall is a security system that monitors and controls incoming and outgoing network traffic based on predetermined security rules. It acts as a barrier between your network and potential threats from the outside world.

Types of Firewalls: There are hardware and software firewalls. A hardware firewall is a physical device that acts as a gatekeeper for network traffic, often included in routers. A software firewall is installed on individual devices and provides additional security by monitoring application-specific traffic.

Configuring Your Firewall: Make sure your firewall is enabled and properly configured to block unauthorized access to your network. Regularly review and update the firewall rules to ensure they meet your current security needs.

Installing Antivirus Software: Antivirus software helps protect your devices from malware and other malicious software. Ensure that antivirus software is installed on all devices connected to your communication hub, and keep it updated to protect against the latest threats.

- **Best Practices for Password Security**

Passwords are a fundamental part of securing your communication hub. Weak or easily guessed passwords can be a significant security vulnerability.

Creating Strong Passwords: Use long passwords with a mix of uppercase and lowercase letters, numbers, and special characters. Avoid common words or easily guessed information like names or birthdays.

Using Two-Factor Authentication (2FA): Two-factor authentication adds an extra layer of security by requiring not just a password but also a second form of verification, such as a code sent to your phone or an authentication app. Enable 2FA on all devices and accounts that support it.

Avoiding Password Reuse: Do not use the same password for multiple devices or accounts. If one password is compromised, it could lead to a breach of all your systems. Consider using a password manager to securely store and manage your passwords.

Regularly Changing Passwords: Change your passwords regularly to reduce the risk of them being compromised. If you suspect that a password has been compromised, change it immediately.

- **Educating Your Family and Team Members**

Cybersecurity is a team effort, especially in a household or group setting. Everyone who has access to your communication hub needs to understand basic security practices.

Teaching Safe Internet Habits: Educate family members and team members about the dangers of clicking on unknown links or downloading attachments from untrusted sources, which can introduce malware into your network.

Recognizing Phishing Attempts: Show examples of phishing emails and messages to help everyone recognize and avoid these scams. Encourage them to report any suspicious communications immediately.

Limiting Access: Only give access to your communication hub and network to those who absolutely need it. Fewer people with access mean fewer opportunities for security breaches.

- **Regular Security Audits and Backups**

Finally, regular maintenance and backups are vital for a secure communication hub.

Conducting Security Audits: Periodically review your security settings, passwords, and devices to ensure everything is secure. Check for any unauthorized devices connected to your network and remove them.

Backing Up Important Data: Regularly back up important data and configuration settings for your communication devices. This ensures that if a device is compromised, you can quickly restore it to a secure state without losing critical information.

Testing Your Security Measures: Simulate cyber threats or run security drills to test how well your communication hub and its users can handle an attempted breach. This will help you identify any weaknesses and improve your security setup.

By implementing these measures, you can significantly reduce the risk of cyber threats to your communication hub. A well-secured hub ensures that your emergency communication remains reliable and trustworthy, giving you peace of mind during critical situations.

CHAPTER 5

Establishing Communication Protocols

Code Words and Signals for Security and Clarity

During emergencies, clear and secure communication is essential for ensuring the safety and coordination of everyone involved. One effective way to achieve this is through the use of code words and signals. These are prearranged phrases or gestures that convey specific messages quickly and without misunderstanding. Code words and signals are particularly valuable when privacy is crucial, such as in situations where you need to communicate discreetly or protect sensitive information from being intercepted.

- **The Importance of Code Words and Signals**

Code words and signals are critical for several reasons:

Security: In a crisis, you may need to share information without revealing it to outsiders. Code words help protect your messages from being easily understood by anyone who might be eavesdropping, whether in person, on a radio, or over a phone line.

Clarity: Emergencies can be chaotic, and emotions can run high. Clear communication is essential to avoid confusion. Code words and signals provide a concise way to convey important information without lengthy explanations.

Speed: When time is of the essence, using a code word or signal can communicate a complex message instantly, allowing for quicker decision-making and actions.

Coordination: Code words and signals ensure that all members of your family or group are on the same page, which is vital for coordinating actions and responses during an emergency.

Preventing Panic: In some situations, you may need to convey critical information without causing panic. Code words allow you to alert specific individuals without alarming others.

- **How to Develop Effective Code Words and Signals**

Creating effective code words and signals requires careful thought and planning. Here are some guidelines to help you develop a system that works for your family or group:

Keep It Simple: Choose words and signals that are easy to remember and pronounce. Avoid complex or unfamiliar words that could lead to confusion during a stressful situation.

Be Specific: Each code word or signal should have a distinct and specific meaning. This avoids ambiguity and ensures that everyone understands exactly what is being communicated.

Use Familiar Terms: Use words and signals that are familiar to everyone in your group. This makes it easier to remember them and reduces the likelihood of mistakes.

Avoid Common Words: Select code words that are not commonly used in everyday conversation. This prevents accidental triggers and reduces the chance of someone guessing the code word's meaning.

Practice Regularly: Regular practice helps ensure that everyone remembers the code words and signals and knows how to use them correctly. Conduct drills to reinforce their use and test everyone's knowledge.

Update as Needed: Review your code words and signals periodically to ensure they are still relevant and effective. Update them if necessary, especially if someone outside your group learns them or if they become outdated.

- **Examples of Code Words and Signals**

Here are some examples of code words and signals that you can use in different emergency situations:

Emergency Evacuation: Use a code word like "Red Sky" to signal that everyone needs to evacuate immediately. This avoids using the word "evacuate," which could cause panic or alert others to your plans.

Check-In or Confirmation: A simple word like "All Clear" can be used to confirm that everyone is safe or that a specific area is secure.

Danger or Threat Alert: Use a phrase like "Code Black" to indicate that there is an immediate danger, such as an intruder or a natural disaster. Everyone who hears this code word knows to take protective action right away.

Medical Emergency: A phrase like "Blue Alert" can signal that someone needs medical assistance without revealing details to others who may overhear the conversation.

Gathering Point: Use a code word like "Meet at the Pine" to direct everyone to a specific safe location, such as a designated meeting spot.

Status Update: A signal like three short bursts on a whistle can indicate a request for a status update, prompting all members to check in and report their situation.

Go Silent: A phrase like "Radio Silence" instructs everyone to stop all communication temporarily, which can be useful if you suspect your communications are being monitored.

- **Using Signals for Non-Verbal Communication**

Sometimes, it's not safe or possible to use verbal communication, especially if you're in a situation where noise could attract unwanted attention or if you're using a radio that could be intercepted. In such cases, non-verbal signals can be incredibly useful. These signals can include gestures, light signals, or sounds.

Hand Signals: Develop a set of hand signals that everyone in your group understands. For example, raising your hand with all five fingers spread could mean "Stop," while pointing two fingers to your eyes and then outwards could mean "I see something."

Flashlight Signals: In the dark, you can use a flashlight to communicate. For example, three short flashes could mean "I need help," while one long flash could mean "I am okay."

Whistle Blasts: Using a whistle is an effective way to communicate over long distances without using your voice. For example, one blast could mean "Attention," two blasts could mean "Advance," and three blasts could mean "Emergency."

Mirror Flashes: During the day, a small mirror can be used to reflect sunlight and create flashes. These flashes can be used to send signals, particularly over long distances.

- **Teaching and Practicing Code Words and Signals**

Once you've developed your set of code words and signals, it's essential to teach them to everyone who might need to use them. This includes family members, friends, and neighbors who are part of your emergency plan.

Hold a Training Session: Organize a session where everyone can learn and practice the code words and signals. Go over each word and signal's meaning, and discuss different scenarios in which they might be used.

Conduct Drills: Regular drills help reinforce the code words and signals and ensure that everyone knows how to use them correctly. These drills can simulate different emergency situations, allowing everyone to practice using the code words and signals in a realistic setting.

Create Flashcards: For younger children or those who might have difficulty remembering the code words, create flashcards with the word on one side and its meaning on the other. This can be a fun way to learn and remember the code words.

Involve Everyone: Make sure that everyone, regardless of age or ability, understands the code words and signals. Practice with each person individually if needed, and ensure they feel comfortable using the system.

- **Reviewing and Updating Your System**

Over time, your needs and circumstances may change, so it's essential to review and update your code words and signals periodically.

Evaluate Effectiveness: After each drill or real emergency, take time to review the effectiveness of your code words and signals. Did everyone understand and respond correctly? Were there any misunderstandings or delays?

Gather Feedback: Ask everyone involved for feedback on the code words and signals. Are they easy to remember and use? Do any of them need to be changed or clarified?

Make Adjustments: Based on your evaluation and feedback, make any necessary adjustments to your code words and signals. This might involve changing a word, adding a new signal, or simplifying the system.

- **Keeping Your System Confidential**

It's crucial to keep your code words and signals confidential to ensure they remain effective. Only share them with those who need to know, and remind everyone to keep them private. If you suspect that someone outside your group has learned your code words or signals, update them immediately to maintain security.

Using code words and signals is an effective way to enhance security, clarity, and coordination during emergencies. By developing a clear and simple system, practicing regularly, and keeping your system confidential, you can ensure that everyone in your group can communicate effectively and securely, no matter what challenges arise.

When and How to Use Emergency Frequencies

In times of disaster or emergency, reliable communication becomes a lifeline. Emergency frequencies are specific radio channels set aside by authorities worldwide for public use during emergencies. Understanding when and how to use these frequencies is essential for effective communication, coordination, and safety. These frequencies are crucial tools for preppers and anyone involved in emergency preparedness to help maintain contact with family, friends, and emergency responders.

- **What Are Emergency Frequencies?**

Emergency frequencies are designated radio channels that are reserved for emergency communications. These frequencies are monitored by emergency services, such as police, fire departments, medical teams, and rescue organizations, to provide a communication channel during crises. They are crucial for reporting emergencies, coordinating rescue efforts, and disseminating vital information. Emergency frequencies can vary depending on the country and type of service but generally include certain frequencies within the Citizen Band (CB), Family Radio Service (FRS), General Mobile Radio Service (GMRS), and amateur (ham) radio bands.

- **Types of Emergency Frequencies**

There are several types of emergency frequencies that you might use during an emergency:

Citizen Band (CB) Radio Frequencies: CB radios are widely used for short-distance communication and do not require a license in most countries. Channel 9 (27.065 MHz) on the CB radio is designated for emergency communications in many regions. It's a good frequency to monitor for general emergency information or to call for help.

Family Radio Service (FRS) and General Mobile Radio Service (GMRS) Frequencies: FRS radios operate on frequencies between 462 and 467 MHz. These are great for local, short-distance communication among family and friends. Channel 1 (462.5625 MHz) is often used for emergencies. GMRS radios, which require a license in some countries, operate on the same frequencies but can use higher power for longer ranges.

Amateur (Ham) Radio Frequencies: Ham radio operators use a wide range of frequencies that can reach across town, across the country, or even around the world. Specific bands are often designated for emergency use, such as the 2-meter band (144-148 MHz) and the 70-centimeter band (420-450 MHz). Ham radio operators often organize into emergency service groups, such as the Amateur Radio Emergency Service (ARES), that provide communication support during disasters.

NOAA Weather Radio Frequencies: The National Oceanic and Atmospheric Administration (NOAA) Weather Radio broadcasts continuous weather information directly from the nearest National Weather Service office. Frequencies range from 162.400 to 162.550 MHz. These are not used for two-way communication but are vital for receiving weather alerts and warnings during emergencies.

- **When to Use Emergency Frequencies**

Knowing when to use emergency frequencies is just as important as knowing how to use them. Here are some scenarios when it is appropriate to use these frequencies:

Immediate Danger: If you or someone else is in immediate danger due to an injury, fire, natural disaster, or other life-threatening situations, using an emergency frequency can help you quickly connect with first responders.

Natural Disasters: Events such as hurricanes, tornadoes, earthquakes, or floods can disrupt regular communication channels. In these cases, using emergency frequencies can help you receive updates, request help, or coordinate with others.

Search and Rescue: If you are lost, stranded, or part of a search and rescue operation, emergency frequencies provide a way to communicate with rescuers and other teams involved.

Widespread Power Outage: When traditional communication networks (like cell towers) are down due to power outages, emergency frequencies can still be active and provide a means to communicate.

Evacuation Orders: During mandatory evacuations or other public safety alerts, using emergency frequencies can help you stay informed about routes, safe zones, and shelter availability.

- **How to Use Emergency Frequencies**

Proper use of emergency frequencies ensures that they remain available for those who need them most. Here are steps and guidelines on how to use these frequencies effectively:

Identify the Correct Frequency: First, make sure you know which frequency to use. Each service has its specific frequencies reserved for emergencies. For example, if you have a CB radio, you would tune to Channel 9. If you have a ham radio, you would use a designated emergency frequency in your area.

Listen Before Transmitting: Always listen to the frequency before you start transmitting. This is to ensure you do not interrupt an ongoing conversation or emergency communication. If the channel is clear, proceed with your communication.

Use Plain Language: Speak clearly and use plain, simple language. Avoid using jargon or codes that may not be understood by everyone. Your goal is to convey your message as clearly and quickly as possible.

State the Nature of the Emergency: Begin by stating "Emergency" to signal that your communication is urgent. Then, describe the nature of your emergency clearly and concisely. For example, "Emergency, this is Chadwick. We have a medical emergency with an unconscious person at 12 Avenue junction. Requesting immediate assistance."

Provide Detailed Location Information: Give a precise location if possible. This can include landmarks, street names, or GPS coordinates. The more specific you are, the easier it will be for help to find you.

Follow Protocol: If you are a licensed operator, such as a ham radio user, follow the proper communication protocol and use your call sign as required. This helps maintain order and accountability on the airwaves.

Keep Messages Brief: During an emergency, airwaves can become crowded. Keep your messages as brief as possible to allow others to use the frequency as well. Once you have conveyed your message, listen for a response or further instructions.

Acknowledge Responses: If you receive a response, acknowledge it immediately. Confirm that you have received the information or instructions and follow them accordingly.

- **Best Practices for Using Emergency Frequencies**

Using emergency frequencies responsibly ensures that they remain effective tools during crises. Here are some best practices to keep in mind:

Do Not Use for Casual Conversation: Emergency frequencies should never be used for casual conversation or non-emergency communication. This can clog the frequency and prevent those in real need from getting through.

Regularly Test Your Equipment: Make sure your radios and other communication devices are in good working order. Regularly test them on their respective frequencies to ensure they are functioning correctly.

Know the Local Emergency Frequencies: Different regions may have different designated emergency frequencies. Make sure you know the ones relevant to your location, and keep a list handy for quick reference.

Educate Your Family and Group Members: Make sure everyone in your family or group knows when and how to use emergency frequencies.

Practice using the devices and frequencies regularly so that everyone is familiar with the process.

Respect Priority Communications: During a disaster, certain communications may take priority, such as those from emergency responders or coordination centers. Always give priority to these communications and wait for a clear channel before transmitting.

- **Emergency Frequency Etiquette**

Etiquette on emergency frequencies is not just about politeness; it's about ensuring effective communication when it matters most. Here are some key points of etiquette to follow:

Monitor Before You Speak: Always monitor the frequency before speaking to ensure that you are not interrupting an ongoing emergency communication.

Speak Calmly and Clearly: Even in emergencies, it's important to speak in a calm, clear voice. Panic can make your message harder to understand.

Avoid Repeating Messages: If your message has been acknowledged, there is no need to repeat it unless asked to do so. Repetition can congest the frequency.

Sign Off Appropriately: If you no longer need to use the frequency, sign off appropriately to indicate that you are leaving the channel free for others.

Report Malicious Use: If you hear someone misusing the emergency frequencies, report it to the authorities if possible. Misuse can jeopardize the effectiveness of emergency communications.

Emergency frequencies are vital resources in times of crisis, providing a direct line of communication when other methods fail. Knowing when and how to use these frequencies can make a significant difference in how effectively you respond to emergencies. By understanding the types of frequencies available, recognizing when to use them, and following proper usage protocols and etiquette, you can help ensure that these frequencies remain a valuable tool for everyone during a disaster.

Communicating Under Stress

During emergencies, stress levels are often high, which can significantly impact how we communicate. Effective communication under stress is critical, as it can mean the difference between clarity and confusion, or even life and death. Whether you are trying to relay vital information to family members, emergency responders, or your community, it is essential to know how to communicate effectively under pressure. Here are some best practices to help maintain clear and effective communication in stressful situations.

- **Understanding the Impact of Stress on Communication**

Stress can profoundly affect how we communicate. When people are stressed, they may:

Speak Too Quickly or Too Slowly: Under stress, some people rush their words, making them hard to understand, while others might slow down or freeze up.

Use Jumbled or Incoherent Speech: Stress can cause confusion, leading to mixed-up words or sentences that don't make sense.

Raise Their Voice: People often speak louder when stressed, which can be perceived as yelling or anger, adding to the tension of the situation.

Forget Key Information: Stress can impair memory, causing people to forget critical details, such as addresses, names, or important instructions.

Misinterpret Others: High stress can lead to misunderstandings, as people may mishear or misconstrue what is being said due to distraction or heightened emotions.

Understanding these impacts is the first step in preparing to communicate effectively under stress.

- ## Best Practices for Communicating Under Stress

To communicate effectively under stress, it is crucial to use strategies that promote clarity, calmness, and accuracy. Here are several best practices to consider:

Stay Calm and Collected

Remaining calm is the foundation of effective communication under stress. If you feel panicked, take a deep breath and try to collect your thoughts before speaking.

Pause and Breathe: Before speaking, take a moment to inhale deeply and exhale slowly. This simple act can help slow down your heart rate and reduce anxiety.

Ground Yourself: Focus on something in your immediate environment to ground yourself and keep your mind clear. This could be a piece of furniture, a calming image, or even your own breathing.

Use Positive Self-Talk: Remind yourself that staying calm will help you communicate more effectively. Simple affirmations like "I can handle this" or "Stay focused" can make a big difference.

Be Clear and Concise

When communicating under stress, clarity is key. Make sure your message is easy to understand by being direct and to the point.

Use Simple Language: Avoid jargon, technical terms, or complex language that might confuse the listener. Stick to plain, straightforward language.

Stick to the Essentials: Focus on the most important information that needs to be conveyed. Avoid unnecessary details that could complicate or confuse the message.

Repeat Key Points: If the situation allows, repeat the critical parts of your message to ensure they are understood. For example, repeat an address or an instruction twice to confirm clarity.

Use Active Listening

Effective communication is a two-way process that involves both speaking and listening. Active listening ensures that you understand the needs and responses of others.

Give Full Attention: Focus entirely on the person speaking without distractions. This shows respect and ensures you are not missing any critical information.

Acknowledge What You Hear: Nod or use short verbal acknowledgments like "I see" or "Got it" to show that you are following along.

Paraphrase for Clarity: Repeat back what you've heard in your own words to confirm understanding. For example, "So, you're saying we should move to the east side of the building?"

Maintain a Steady Tone and Volume

Your tone and volume can convey a lot more than words. In stressful situations, maintaining a steady tone helps prevent escalation and keeps communication clear.

Avoid Shouting or Whispering: Speak at a normal volume. Shouting can escalate stress, while whispering might make it hard to hear or seem secretive.

Use a Calm and Reassuring Tone: Even if you are feeling stressed, try to keep your voice calm and measured. This helps reassure others and maintain a composed atmosphere.

Pace Yourself: Speak at a moderate pace—not too fast or too slow. This helps ensure your message is clear and prevents misunderstandings.

Avoid Misinformation and Speculation

In an emergency, the accuracy of information is crucial. Misinformation or speculation can lead to panic, confusion, and dangerous decisions.

Stick to the Facts: Only share information that you are sure of. If you do not know something, it is better to say, "I'm not sure" than to guess.

Clarify Uncertain Information: If you are uncertain about a piece of information, clarify it with someone who knows. This prevents the spread of rumors and maintains trust.

Avoid Assumptions: Do not assume others know what you know. Be clear and explicit in your communication to avoid misunderstandings.

Practice Patience and Empathy

Stressful situations can be overwhelming for everyone involved. Being patient and empathetic can help de-escalate tension and foster better communication.

Be Patient with Others: Understand that others may also be under stress and might need time to gather their thoughts or repeat their message.

Show Empathy: Acknowledge the emotions of others. Simple phrases like, "I understand this is hard," can help others feel heard and valued.

Stay Supportive: Encourage and support others in stressful situations. Positive reinforcement can help calm nerves and keep everyone focused on the task.

Prepare and Practice Regularly

Preparation can significantly improve your ability to communicate under stress. Knowing what to do in advance makes it easier to stay calm and clear.

Create a Communication Plan: Have a plan in place for different emergency scenarios. Know who to contact, what information to share, and the best communication methods to use.

Regularly Practice Drills: Conduct regular emergency communication drills with your family or group. Practicing under simulated stress can help everyone become more comfortable with the process.

Keep a List of Key Information: Maintain a readily accessible list of critical information, such as contact numbers, addresses, and emergency protocols. Having this information on hand can reduce stress during an actual emergency.

Use Visual Aids and Tools

Visual aids and tools can enhance understanding, especially when stress might cloud verbal communication.

Use Hand Signals: In noisy environments or when verbal communication is difficult, hand signals can be an effective way to convey messages quickly and clearly.

Employ Written Notes: If possible, write down important information or instructions. This can help others who may not have heard or understood verbal communication due to stress.

Use Maps and Diagrams: Visual tools like maps and diagrams can help clarify directions or plans, especially when giving complex instructions.

- **Why Effective Communication Under Stress Matters**

Communicating effectively under stress is crucial because it helps ensure safety, provides reassurance, and enables effective coordination during emergencies. Clear communication prevents misunderstandings, helps in accurate decision-making, and facilitates faster and more organized responses. Moreover, maintaining a calm demeanor and providing clear instructions can help reduce the anxiety and fear of those around you, creating a more controlled and manageable environment.

Effective communication under stress is not just a skill but a critical component of emergency preparedness. By staying calm, being clear and concise, actively listening, avoiding misinformation, showing empathy, and preparing in advance, you can significantly improve your ability to communicate in high-pressure situations. These practices help ensure that you, your family, and your community can respond effectively during emergencies, keeping everyone safer and more informed. Practicing these strategies regularly will help make them second nature, so they become automatic responses in a crisis.

CHAPTER 6

Staying Informed: Receiving Emergency Alerts and Updates

Understanding Emergency Alert Systems (EAS)

Emergency Alert Systems (EAS) are vital tools designed to keep the public informed and safe during emergencies. These systems are used to broadcast warnings and critical information about various threats, such as natural disasters, terrorist attacks, or technological hazards. Knowing how EAS works and how to utilize it effectively can help preppers stay informed and make timely decisions during a disaster.

- **What Are Emergency Alert Systems (EAS)**

Emergency Alert Systems are networks established by the government to quickly disseminate urgent information to the public. These systems are designed to provide timely warnings and instructions to people in affected areas.

Here's how EAS functions:

Broadcast Alerts: EAS sends alerts through various broadcast channels, including radio, television, cable systems, and satellite radio and television providers. When an alert is issued, it interrupts regular programming to deliver the emergency message.

Targeted Messaging: The alerts are targeted geographically, meaning they are only broadcasted to the regions affected by the emergency. This ensures that people who need the information receive it promptly.

Types of Alerts: EAS can deliver different types of alerts, ranging from weather warnings (like tornado or hurricane alerts) to AMBER alerts for missing children and alerts for public safety emergencies, such as chemical spills or terrorist threats.

EAS is managed jointly by various federal, state, and local agencies, including the Federal Emergency Management Agency (FEMA), the Federal Communications Commission (FCC), and the National Oceanic and Atmospheric Administration (NOAA).

- **How Do Emergency Alert Systems Work?**

Understanding how EAS works can help preppers use this tool effectively. The system operates through a coordinated network of federal, state, and local agencies that issue alerts based on specific criteria.

Alert Origination: An alert is initiated by an authorized government agency, such as the National Weather Service (NWS) for weather-related alerts or local law enforcement for AMBER alerts.

Broadcast Interruption: When an alert is activated, EAS automatically interrupts regular broadcasts on television and radio to deliver the message. This ensures that people who are tuned into these channels are immediately informed of the emergency.

Digital and Wireless Alerts: In addition to traditional broadcast methods, EAS also works with the Wireless Emergency Alerts (WEA) system, which sends messages directly to mobile phones. This technology is particularly useful for reaching people who may not be near a TV or radio when an alert is issued.

Message Content: EAS messages typically provide information about the nature of the emergency, the areas affected, and instructions on what actions to take. For example, during a tornado warning, the alert might advise people to take cover in a safe location.

The effectiveness of EAS depends on the cooperation and readiness of broadcasters, cable operators, and other media outlets to ensure timely and accurate dissemination of alerts.

- **How Preppers Can Use EAS to Stay Informed**

For preppers, staying informed during a disaster is crucial. EAS provides a reliable source of real-time information that can help preppers make informed decisions. Here are some ways preppers can utilize EAS:

1. Invest in Reliable Equipment

To take full advantage of EAS, preppers should have the right equipment to receive alerts.

NOAA Weather Radios: These radios are specifically designed to receive alerts from the National Weather Service. They can be set to sound an alarm when an alert is issued, ensuring that you receive notifications even when you are asleep or otherwise occupied.

Portable AM/FM Radios: A battery-operated or hand-crank radio can also receive EAS alerts, making it an essential piece of equipment for any prepper's emergency kit.

Smartphones with WEA Capability: Ensure your smartphone is set up to receive Wireless Emergency Alerts (WEA). These alerts are sent directly to your phone and do not require an internet connection, which is ideal when traditional communication networks are down.

2. Understand the Different Types of Alerts

Knowing what different types of alerts mean can help preppers respond appropriately.

Weather Alerts: These include warnings for tornadoes, hurricanes, floods, and severe thunderstorms. Preppers should understand the differences between a watch (conditions are favorable for an event) and a warning (an event is imminent or occurring).

AMBER Alerts: Issued for missing children, these alerts are broadcasted to raise public awareness. While not a direct threat, being aware of AMBER alerts helps preppers stay informed about activities in their area.

Civil Emergency Alerts: These alerts notify the public of significant emergencies, such as terrorist attacks, chemical spills, or large-scale evacuations. Preppers should be prepared to act immediately when these alerts are issued, following instructions to shelter in place or evacuate.

3. Regularly Monitor Alert Systems

Preppers should regularly monitor alert systems to stay updated on any potential threats.

Keep Radios Tuned to Local Stations: Maintain a habit of listening to local radio stations, especially during severe weather seasons or when a known threat is present. This ensures that you receive any alerts as soon as they are issued.

Check Alert Apps and Websites: There are several apps and websites that provide real-time updates on alerts. Preppers should have reliable apps installed on their smartphones and bookmark relevant websites for quick access.

4. Plan and Practice Responses

Having a plan in place for different types of alerts can save time and reduce stress during an actual emergency.

Create an Action Plan: For each type of alert, determine what actions need to be taken. This might include moving to a storm shelter during a tornado warning or evacuating during a wildfire alert.

Conduct Regular Drills: Practice your response to different alerts with your family. This ensures everyone knows what to do and can act quickly and calmly.

Stay Updated on Local Plans: Understand the emergency plans of your local community, such as evacuation routes or shelter locations. This information is often included in emergency alerts and can be critical during a disaster.

- **The Importance of EAS for Preppers**

Emergency Alert Systems provide an essential service, especially for preppers who prioritize staying informed and ready for any situation. By understanding how EAS works and integrating its alerts into your preparedness plans, you can enhance your readiness for emergencies.

Benefits of Using EAS

Timely Information: EAS ensures that preppers receive the latest information about potential threats and hazards, allowing for swift and informed decision-making.

Wide Reach: With the ability to broadcast alerts over multiple platforms, including radio, television, and mobile devices, EAS can reach preppers wherever they are.

Reliability: Because EAS operates on a range of platforms and is managed by various agencies, it provides a dependable source of information even when other communication methods fail.

- **Challenges and Limitations**

While EAS is a powerful tool, it does have some limitations:

Dependent on Infrastructure: EAS relies on broadcast and mobile networks, which can be affected by power outages or damage to infrastructure during a disaster.

Geographic Limitations: Some remote areas may have limited access to broadcast signals, reducing the effectiveness of EAS in those locations.

Message Clarity: EAS messages need to be concise, which can sometimes lead to a lack of detailed instructions or explanations.

Despite these challenges, EAS remains a critical component of emergency preparedness for preppers. By understanding its functionality, preparing the right equipment, and integrating its alerts into your preparedness strategies, you can better protect yourself and your loved ones in times of crisis.

Emergency Alert Systems are a cornerstone of public safety, providing timely and targeted alerts to keep people informed during emergencies. For preppers, understanding and utilizing EAS is vital for effective disaster preparedness. By investing in the right equipment, staying informed about different types of alerts, and practicing responses, preppers can enhance their readiness and ensure they are always prepared for whatever comes their way.

NOAA Weather Radios and Their Importance

NOAA Weather Radios are essential tools in emergency preparedness. They provide real-time weather information, warnings, and alerts, helping families stay safe during severe weather events. Understanding how NOAA Weather Radios work, how to use them, and why they are crucial can enhance your preparedness strategy, ensuring you receive timely and accurate information when it matters most.

What Are NOAA Weather Radios?

NOAA Weather Radios are special types of radios that continuously broadcast weather information directly from the National Oceanic and Atmospheric Administration (NOAA) National Weather Service (NWS). These radios operate on seven different frequencies reserved exclusively for weather information and emergency broadcasts, providing a 24-hour, reliable source of weather data. Unlike standard AM/FM radios, NOAA Weather Radios can alert you to severe weather and other hazards in your area, even if you're not actively listening.

Key features of NOAA Weather Radios include:

Continuous Broadcast: They provide round-the-clock weather updates and emergency information.

Tone Alert Feature: Many NOAA Weather Radios are equipped with a tone alert feature that automatically sounds an alarm and turns on the radio when a severe weather alert is issued.

Battery Backup: These radios often have a battery backup option, ensuring they work during power outages.

Specific Area Message Encoding (SAME) Technology: This technology allows you to program your radio to receive alerts specific to your local area, reducing unnecessary alerts for regions far from your location.

- **Importance of NOAA Weather Radios in Emergency Preparedness**

NOAA Weather Radios play a vital role in keeping you informed about potential weather threats and other emergencies. Here's why they are a key component of any emergency preparedness plan:

Immediate Alerts and Warnings: Unlike other sources of weather information, NOAA Weather Radios can provide immediate alerts as soon as they are issued by the NWS. This is crucial during severe weather events, such as tornadoes, hurricanes, or flash floods, where every second counts for taking shelter or evacuating.

Reliable Communication Source: In many emergencies, standard communication networks can fail due to power outages, infrastructure damage, or network overload. NOAA Weather Radios use dedicated frequencies that remain operational even when other systems are down, making them a reliable source of information when you need it most.

Geographically Targeted Alerts: With the SAME technology, NOAA Weather Radios can be programmed to receive alerts specific to your area, ensuring you are not overwhelmed with alerts irrelevant to your location. This feature is particularly useful in regions where weather conditions can vary widely over short distances.

Awareness of Multiple Hazards: Beyond weather events, NOAA Weather Radios also broadcast alerts for other emergencies, including natural disasters (like earthquakes), technological incidents (such as chemical spills), and public safety threats (like AMBER alerts). This makes them versatile tools for comprehensive emergency preparedness.

Accessibility and Inclusivity: NOAA Weather Radios are accessible to a wide range of users, including those who might not have internet access or smartphones. They are also equipped with features like tone alerts and visual signals, making them useful for people with hearing or vision impairments.

- **How to Use NOAA Weather Radios**

To maximize the benefits of a NOAA Weather Radio, it's essential to know how to use it effectively. Here are some tips and best practices for using these radios:

1. Selecting the Right Radio

Check for SAME Technology: Choose a NOAA Weather Radio with SAME technology to receive alerts specific to your county or area. This feature ensures you only get alerts relevant to your immediate location.

Look for Multiple Power Options: Radios with battery backups, hand cranks, or solar power options are ideal for ensuring you have access to alerts even if the power goes out.

Consider Portability: A portable NOAA Weather Radio can be taken with you during evacuations, camping, or when traveling, ensuring you stay informed no matter where you are.

2. Programming Your Radio

Set Your Location: Use the SAME feature to program your radio for your specific county or location. This process typically involves entering a code for your area, which can be found on the NOAA website or the radio's manual.

Adjust Alert Settings: Customize your alert settings to prioritize the types of alerts most important to you. Some radios allow you to disable alerts for less severe weather conditions if you only want to be notified of significant threats.

3. Placement and Testing

Choose an Optimal Location: Place your NOAA Weather Radio in a central location in your home, where the alert tone can be heard from multiple rooms. Consider keeping a radio in your bedroom to ensure you hear alerts at night.

Regularly Test Your Radio: Conduct monthly tests to ensure your NOAA Weather Radio is working correctly. This involves checking the battery life, ensuring it picks up the local NOAA broadcast, and confirming the alert tone sounds as expected.

4. Responding to Alerts

Understand Alert Types: Familiarize yourself with the different types of alerts, such as watches, warnings, and advisories, and know the appropriate actions to take for each. For example, a "watch" means conditions are favorable for a particular type of weather, while a "warning" indicates that the weather event is imminent or already occurring.

Practice Emergency Drills: Regularly practice your emergency response plan with your family, including what to do when a NOAA Weather Radio alert sounds. This helps ensure everyone knows their roles and can act quickly and calmly during an actual emergency.

Best Practices for NOAA Weather Radio Usage

To make the most of your NOAA Weather Radio, consider incorporating the following best practices into your emergency preparedness plan:

Keep Extra Batteries Handy: If your NOAA Weather Radio operates on batteries, make sure you have extra batteries stored in a safe, accessible location. This ensures you can keep the radio running even during extended power outages.

Use Multiple Alerts: While NOAA Weather Radios are highly reliable, it's a good idea to use them in conjunction with other alert systems, such as smartphone apps or community alert systems. This provides redundancy and ensures you receive alerts even if one system fails.

Educate Family Members: Ensure all family members understand how to use the NOAA Weather Radio, including how to turn it on, interpret alerts, and respond accordingly. This knowledge is particularly important if you're away and cannot assist them during an emergency.

Stay Informed About Updates: Occasionally, check the NOAA website or contact your local National Weather Service office to stay updated on any changes to alert codes, frequencies, or new features that may enhance your radio's functionality.

- **The Versatility of NOAA Weather Radios**

NOAA Weather Radios are versatile tools for emergency preparedness, providing more than just weather alerts. They also serve as:

Information Sources During Blackouts: In extended power outages, these radios can keep you informed about when services might be restored or when evacuation orders are lifted.

Portable Safety Devices: Lightweight and easy to carry, NOAA Weather Radios can be taken on trips, making them ideal for outdoor adventures or travel in unfamiliar areas prone to severe weather.

Community Alert Networks: Some communities use NOAA Weather Radios to relay local alerts, such as school closures or boil water advisories, making them useful even beyond severe weather events.

Incorporating NOAA Weather Radios into your emergency preparedness plan is a simple yet effective way to enhance your ability to respond to various threats. These radios provide timely, reliable, and geographically targeted alerts, ensuring you have the information needed to make critical safety decisions during an emergency. By choosing the right radio, programming it correctly, and following best practices, you can maximize the benefits of this essential tool, keeping yourself and your loved ones safe and informed no matter what challenges come your way.

Utilizing Local Networks and Social Media Responsibly

In today's digital age, local networks and social media have become powerful tools for sharing information, especially during emergencies. These platforms allow people to receive real-time updates, connect with neighbors, and provide mutual support. However, using these tools effectively requires understanding how to filter reliable information, avoid spreading rumors, and protect privacy and security.

Understanding Local Networks and Social Media in Emergencies

Local networks include neighborhood groups, community organizations, and local news outlets that provide updates specific to your area. Social media platforms such as Facebook, Twitter, Instagram, and Nextdoor can be used to access this information and share it quickly. During emergencies, these channels can offer:

Real-Time Updates: Immediate information on the situation, including weather updates, road closures, and emergency services' activities.

Community Support: A way to connect with neighbors and share resources, such as shelter locations, food supplies, or medical help.

Crowdsourced Information: Reports from community members about conditions in various parts of town, which can help others make informed decisions about travel or safety.

- **Using Local Networks Responsibly**

1. Join Local Community Groups

Neighborhood Watch Groups: Many communities have neighborhood watch programs or similar groups that share information about local safety and emergency preparedness. Joining these groups can keep you informed about potential threats and community responses.

Community Apps and Websites: Platforms like Nextdoor are specifically designed for neighborhoods. You can use these to connect with neighbors, share alerts, and access local resources.

Make sure to check for your local city or county emergency management websites, as they often have official alerts and updates.

2. Follow Reliable Local Sources

Local Government and News Outlets: Make sure to follow your local government's social media accounts and trusted news outlets. These sources are more likely to provide accurate and timely information compared to personal accounts.

Emergency Services: Police, fire departments, and other emergency services often have social media profiles where they post updates. Following these accounts ensures you get accurate information directly from the source.

Engage in Community Drills and Education Programs

Participate in Drills: Engage in local emergency drills and training exercises. Many communities host these events to prepare residents for various scenarios, and they often use social media and local networks to share information and coordinate.

Educational Programs: Join local programs that teach emergency preparedness, first aid, or disaster response. These programs frequently have associated social media groups where members share tips, news, and updates.

- **Using Social Media Responsibly**

1. Verify Information Before Sharing

Check Multiple Sources: Before sharing any post or news about an emergency, check multiple sources to confirm its accuracy. Spreading false information can cause panic and confusion.

Avoid Sensationalism: Stick to sharing facts and official updates. Avoid posts that use emotional language or that seem designed to incite fear or anger, as these are often less reliable.

Consider the Source: Be cautious of posts from unknown or unreliable sources. Even well-meaning friends may inadvertently share incorrect information. Look for posts from official accounts or those that cite credible news organizations or government entities.

2. Maintain Privacy and Security

Avoid Sharing Personal Information: Be mindful not to share sensitive information, such as your exact location, family details, or plans, which could be misused. This is especially important during evacuations or in unstable situations.

Use Secure Platforms: Some platforms offer more privacy and security features than others. Familiarize yourself with these features, such as private groups, encrypted messaging, or anonymity settings, to protect your personal information.

3. Encourage Positive Community Interaction

Support Constructive Dialogue: Encourage calm and respectful communication. In emergencies, stress levels are high, and tensions can flare. Keeping discussions focused on solutions and support rather than blame or criticism fosters a more helpful community atmosphere.

Share Helpful Resources: Use social media to share useful information, such as lists of local shelters, contacts for emergency services, or advice on staying safe. Providing resources can help others feel prepared and reduce anxiety.

- **Avoiding the Spread of Misinformation**

Understand the Impact of Misinformation

Causes Panic: False information can lead to unnecessary panic, causing people to make dangerous decisions, such as evacuating unnecessarily or ignoring legitimate warnings.

Wastes Resources: Misinformation can lead to the misuse of emergency services, diverting resources away from real emergencies to deal with false alarms.

2. Check for Official Confirmation

Look for Verification: Always check if the information has been confirmed by an official source, such as local government websites, verified news outlets, or emergency services.

Beware of Outdated Information: Some emergencies evolve quickly, and what was true an hour ago may no longer be accurate. Double-check the time stamps on posts and updates to ensure you're acting on current information.

3. Educate Others on Responsible Sharing

Promote Critical Thinking: Encourage your community to think critically about the information they see online. Discuss how to recognize reliable sources and why it's important to avoid spreading rumors.

Lead by Example: Be a role model in your community by only sharing verified, helpful information and by correcting misinformation when you see it.

- Building a Strong Community Network

1. Form a Community Response Team

Organize a Team: Form a local emergency response team composed of neighbors and community members trained in basic emergency response skills. Use social media to coordinate meetings and share training resources.

Set Up Communication Channels: Establish dedicated communication channels, like group texts or private social media groups, for sharing information and coordinating during emergencies.

2. Coordinate with Local Authorities

Stay in Contact with Local Officials: Establish a line of communication with local emergency management offices and first responders. Keeping them informed about community efforts and needs can improve overall response and resource allocation.

Align with Community Plans: Make sure your community's emergency plans are in sync with local government plans. This alignment ensures that efforts are complementary and not counterproductive.

3. Encourage Preparedness Education

Share Resources and Training: Use local networks and social media to share information on emergency preparedness, such as lists of supplies, first aid instructions, and links to local emergency training sessions.

Host Workshops and Meetings: Organize regular community meetings or workshops focused on preparedness, using social media to promote these events and share outcomes.

- **Balancing Social Media Use During Emergencies**

1. Limit Screen Time

Avoid Over-Checking: Constantly checking social media can increase anxiety and stress. Set specific times to check for updates and stick to them to maintain a sense of calm and focus.

Practice Digital Detox: Occasionally, step away from screens to focus on immediate surroundings and responsibilities. Ensure you're not overwhelmed by the constant flow of information.

2. Monitor Children's Access

Filter Content for Children: Children can easily become frightened by the content they see online. Ensure their social media use is monitored, and guide them towards age-appropriate, factual information.

Discuss What They See: Talk to children about the information they come across on social media, helping them to understand what's real, what's speculation, and how to process these details constructively.

Local networks and social media are invaluable tools during emergencies, offering timely updates, community support, and a platform for sharing resources. However, using these tools responsibly is crucial to avoid spreading misinformation, maintaining privacy, and fostering a supportive community atmosphere. By following best practices, verifying information before sharing, and engaging constructively, you can ensure that these tools are used to their full potential, helping you and your community stay safe and well-informed during emergencies.

CHAPTER 7

Overcoming Communication Barriers

Handling Communication Breakdowns

In an emergency, clear and reliable communication is crucial. However, there are many challenges that can cause communication breakdowns, such as technical failures or misunderstandings. These breakdowns can lead to confusion, misinformation, and even jeopardize safety. Understanding how to handle these issues effectively ensures that you and your family remain connected and informed during critical situations.

- **Understanding Communication Breakdowns**

Communication breakdowns can occur due to several reasons:

Technical Failures: This includes problems like power outages, network failures, broken devices, or poor signal strength.

Misunderstandings: Misinterpretation of messages, unclear instructions, or language barriers can cause confusion.

Environmental Factors: Natural disasters, physical obstructions, and noise pollution can hinder clear communication.

Recognizing these barriers helps in planning ahead to minimize their impact.

- **Strategies to Overcome Technical Failures**

1. Have Backup Communication Tools

Multiple Devices: Always have more than one communication device available. For instance, if a mobile phone fails, a battery-powered radio or a satellite phone can serve as alternatives.

Two-Way Radios: Handheld radios such as FRS/GMRS or Ham radios are reliable for short-range communication, especially when cell networks are down. Ensure these radios are fully charged and that everyone knows how to use them.

2. Maintain Power Sources

Solar Chargers and Power Banks: Keep solar chargers and portable power banks as part of your emergency kit to recharge phones and other small devices during power outages.

Generators: If possible, invest in a generator to provide power to essential communication devices. Ensure you have enough fuel stored safely to run the generator for an extended period.

3. Use Reliable Communication Channels

Prioritize Low-Bandwidth Tools: When the network is congested or weak, use tools that require minimal data, such as text messaging instead of voice or video calls.

Emergency Frequencies: Familiarize yourself with local emergency radio frequencies. These channels are often more reliable than regular communication methods during disasters.

4. Regular Equipment Checks and Maintenance

Routine Testing: Regularly test all communication equipment to ensure it is functioning correctly. Replace batteries and update software as needed.

Device Repairs: Learn basic repairs for your communication devices, such as replacing batteries or antennas, to ensure they remain operational.

- **Overcoming Misunderstandings in Communication**

1. Establish Clear Communication Protocols

Use Simple Language: Communicate using clear and simple language, avoiding jargon or complex terms that might confuse others, especially children.

Repeat Key Information: Encourage repeating critical messages to confirm understanding. For example, when giving instructions, ask the recipient to repeat the steps back to you.

2. Implement Code Words and Signals

Develop a Set of Code Words: Create a list of code words or phrases that are agreed upon within your group. This helps convey essential messages quickly and securely. For instance, use a code word for "safe" or "evacuate" that everyone understands.

Visual Signals: Establish visual signals, like hand signs or colored flags, that can convey messages when verbal communication is not possible.

3. Regular Drills and Practice

Practice Scenarios: Regularly practice different emergency scenarios with your family or group to ensure everyone knows what to do and how to communicate effectively under stress.

Role-Playing: Engage in role-playing exercises to practice responding to various communication breakdowns, such as handling a situation where a device fails or someone misinterprets an instruction.

4. Document Communication Procedures

Create a Communication Plan: Write down a communication plan outlining who to contact, the order of communication, and the primary and backup methods to use. Ensure everyone in the family or group has a copy.

Emergency Contact List: Maintain a list of emergency contacts, including phone numbers, email addresses, and any other relevant details. This list should be easily accessible and updated regularly.

- **Addressing Environmental and Physical Barriers**

1. Choose Appropriate Communication Locations

Seek Higher Ground: If possible, move to higher ground to get a better signal for mobile devices or radios.

Minimize Noise Interference: Find a quiet place away from loud noises to enhance the clarity of your communication, whether you are using a phone, radio, or shouting instructions.

2. Use Physical Communication Aids

Whistles and Signal Mirrors: Include whistles and signal mirrors in your emergency kit. These can be used to attract attention over long distances or in noisy environments.

Visual Cues: Flashlights or other light sources can be used to send visual signals at night or in dark areas. Pre-agree on what specific flashes or patterns mean within your group.

3. Adapt to Environmental Changes

Adapt Your Methods: Be ready to adapt your communication methods based on the environment. For example, in a dense forest, radio signals may be weak, so having a secondary plan, like using whistles, is essential.

Know Your Area: Familiarize yourself with your local environment. Knowing areas with good reception and potential physical barriers will help you better plan your communication strategies.

- **Building Resilience Against Communication Breakdowns**

1. Stay Calm and Focused

Maintain Composure: In a breakdown, staying calm is crucial. Take deep breaths and focus on the most critical task first; restoring communication.

Prioritize Communication Needs: Assess the situation and prioritize communication needs. Decide if you need to communicate immediately or if there is time to find alternative solutions.

2. Have a Contingency Plan

Create Multiple Backup Plans: Develop several communication backup plans and ensure everyone knows what to do if the primary method fails. This could include meeting at a pre-agreed location if all communication fails.

Evaluate and Update Plans: Regularly review and update your communication plans to incorporate new technology or changes in your environment or group.

3. Leverage Community Resources

Local Networks and Community Groups: Engage with local networks and community groups to establish reliable communication channels. Collaborate on shared resources, such as community radios or designated meeting points.

Community Drills: Participate in community emergency drills to practice large-scale communication and coordination, helping identify potential breakdown points in advance.

4. Educate and Empower Everyone

Training and Knowledge Sharing: Educate all group members, including children, on how to use all available communication devices and protocols. Knowledge and preparedness can significantly reduce the impact of communication breakdowns.

Encourage Self-Reliance: Teach each person basic troubleshooting skills for communication devices and emphasize the importance of self-reliance in emergencies.

Communication breakdowns are inevitable during emergencies, but with proper planning and preparation, their impact can be minimized. By understanding potential barriers and implementing strategies to overcome them, such as having backup communication tools, establishing clear protocols, and practicing regularly, you can ensure that you remain connected and informed, even in the most challenging situations. Remember, the key to overcoming communication breakdowns is flexibility, adaptability, and a proactive approach to preparedness.

Strategies for Communicating with Vulnerable Populations

Effective communication during emergencies is essential for everyone, but it becomes particularly critical when dealing with vulnerable populations such as children, the elderly, and people with disabilities. These groups often face additional challenges in understanding, processing, and responding to information, making it crucial to adapt communication strategies to meet their specific needs.

- **Understanding the Needs of Vulnerable Populations**

1. Children

Developmental Considerations: Children may not fully understand complex information or the seriousness of a situation. They often rely on adults for guidance and may feel frightened or confused.

Attention Span: Children generally have shorter attention spans, which means that information needs to be delivered in short, clear, and engaging ways.

2. Elderly Individuals

Sensory Limitations: Many elderly individuals experience hearing or vision impairments, which can make receiving information more challenging.

Cognitive Decline: Some older adults may have memory issues or cognitive impairments, making it harder for them to process and retain information.

Mobility Issues: Physical limitations can hinder an elderly person's ability to respond quickly or reach safety in an emergency.

3. People with Disabilities

Physical Disabilities: Individuals with mobility issues may have difficulty accessing information or reaching safe locations.

Cognitive and Intellectual Disabilities: These individuals may struggle with understanding and processing information, making it essential to use simplified language and repetition.

Sensory Disabilities: Those who are deaf, hard of hearing, blind, or have low vision require alternative methods of communication, such as sign language, braille, or assistive technologies.

- **Effective Communication Strategies for Vulnerable Populations**

1. Use Clear and Simple Language

Avoid Jargon: Communicate in plain language, avoiding technical terms, acronyms, or complex sentences. For example, instead of saying "evacuate immediately," you might say "Leave now. It's not safe here."

Short, Direct Instructions: Give instructions in small, manageable steps. Break down complex tasks into simple actions, such as "Take your emergency bag," "Hold my hand," and "Walk quickly to the door."

2. Leverage Visual Aids and Demonstrations

Visuals for Clarity: Use pictures, diagrams, and color-coded charts to convey information, especially for children and those with cognitive disabilities. Visual aids can simplify complex ideas and make them easier to understand.

Demonstrations: Show rather than tell. For example, physically demonstrate how to put on a life vest or use an emergency radio, rather than just explaining it verbally.

3. Involve Caregivers and Support Systems

Family and Caregiver Involvement: Involve caregivers, family members, or trusted individuals in the communication process. They can help relay information in a way that is familiar and comforting to the vulnerable individual.

Communication Plans: Develop specific communication plans that include contact information for caregivers and protocols for how to communicate with the vulnerable person if their primary caregiver is unavailable.

4. Utilize Technology and Assistive Devices

Assistive Communication Tools: Use devices like hearing aids, text-to-speech software, and braille displays to ensure that people with sensory disabilities receive information. For example, text alerts should be paired with audio notifications for those who are hard of hearing.

Mobile Apps: There are several apps designed to assist in communication with vulnerable populations. Apps like "Be My Eyes" for the visually impaired or "Proloquo2Go" for non-verbal individuals can be invaluable during emergencies.

5. Personalize Communication Approaches

Adapt to the Individual: Tailor your communication strategy to the specific needs of each individual. Some elderly people may prefer written instructions, while others may need spoken words repeated slowly. Similarly, some children may respond better to storytelling or games that convey the message.

Sensitivity and Patience: Be patient and allow extra time for questions. Listen carefully to any concerns and clarify information as needed. This is especially important when communicating with those who may take longer to process information.

6. Pre-Plan and Practice

Emergency Drills: Conduct regular emergency drills that involve vulnerable populations. Practice not just the actions they need to take but also the communication methods you will use. This helps familiarize them with what to expect and reduces anxiety during an actual emergency.

Repetition and Reinforcement: Repetition is key, especially for those with cognitive disabilities or young children. Reinforce the important messages regularly, and make sure they understand what actions to take.

7. Create Accessible Emergency Information

Braille and Large Print: Ensure that all written materials are available in accessible formats, such as large print for the visually impaired and braille for those who are blind.

Sign Language and Captioning: For those who are deaf or hard of hearing, provide information through sign language interpreters or ensure that videos and announcements are captioned.

8. Establish Emergency Contact Systems

Buddy Systems: Implement a buddy system where each vulnerable individual has someone assigned to check in on them regularly during an emergency. This person can help relay information and ensure that the individual's needs are met.

Special Registries: Some communities have special needs registries where individuals with disabilities can register to receive tailored assistance during emergencies. Encourage participation in these programs.

9. Engage Community Resources

Partner with Local Organizations: Work with local organizations that serve vulnerable populations to develop communication strategies. These organizations can offer insights into the best practices for reaching and assisting their clients.

Community Alerts and Networks: Ensure that local emergency alert systems are inclusive and consider the needs of vulnerable populations.

Engage with community leaders to disseminate information through trusted channels.

10. Empower Vulnerable Individuals

Self-Advocacy Training: Teach vulnerable individuals self-advocacy skills. For instance, children can learn how to recognize and signal when they need help, and people with disabilities can be trained on how to use emergency communication tools.

Emergency Kits with Instructions: Provide emergency kits with clear, easy-to-understand instructions. For example, the kit could include flashcards with simple steps on what to do in various scenarios.

- **Special Considerations for Each Group**

1. Children

Interactive Communication: Engage children with interactive methods such as games, songs, or storytelling to teach them emergency procedures.

Reassurance and Comfort: Provide reassurance and comfort during the communication process. Children are highly sensitive to stress and need emotional support to understand and act on information.

2. Elderly

Speak Clearly and Slowly: When communicating with elderly individuals, speak clearly and at a moderate pace. Avoid shouting but ensure your voice is loud enough to be heard.

Check for Understanding: Ask questions to verify that the elderly person understands what is being communicated. Encourage them to ask questions if they're unsure.

3. People with Disabilities

Accessible Locations and Equipment: Ensure that communication happens in locations that are accessible to people with disabilities. This includes spaces that accommodate wheelchairs and other mobility aids.

Assistive Technology: Be familiar with and use any assistive technology the individual might rely on. This can include anything from voice-assisted devices to sign language interpretation.

Effective communication with vulnerable populations during emergencies is not just about delivering information but doing so in a way that is accessible, clear, and considerate of their unique needs. Whether it's through simplifying language for children, using assistive devices for those with disabilities, or ensuring that elderly individuals receive information in an understandable format, tailoring your approach is key to ensuring that everyone remains safe and informed. By incorporating these strategies, you can help bridge the communication gap and provide the necessary support to those who need it most during critical situations.

Dealing with Language Barriers and Disabilities

Emergencies can create chaotic situations where clear communication becomes vital. However, language barriers and disabilities can make it challenging for everyone to understand instructions, warnings, and critical information. It is crucial to adopt effective strategies to ensure that everyone, regardless of language proficiency or ability, can access the information they need to stay safe. This section explores various solutions for overcoming language barriers and communicating effectively with individuals with disabilities during emergencies.

- **Understanding the Challenges**

1. Language Barriers

Diverse Populations: Many communities are linguistically diverse, with residents who may not speak or understand the primary language used for emergency communications. This can lead to misunderstandings and delays in responding to emergency situations.

Limited Language Proficiency: Some individuals may have a basic understanding of the primary language but may struggle with complex terminology or rapid speech, especially under stress.

2. Disabilities

Physical Disabilities: Individuals with mobility impairments may face challenges accessing certain information if it is only available in specific locations or formats.

Sensory Disabilities: People who are deaf, hard of hearing, blind, or have low vision require alternative forms of communication to access emergency alerts and instructions.

Cognitive and Intellectual Disabilities: These individuals may have difficulty processing information quickly or understanding complex instructions, requiring simplified communication methods.

- **Strategies for Overcoming Language Barriers**

1. Multilingual Communication

Provide Information in Multiple Languages: Ensure that all emergency communications are available in the most common languages spoken within the community. This includes written materials, audio messages, and visual aids.

Translation Services: Utilize translation services to convert emergency information into multiple languages. This can be done in advance for pre-planned emergency procedures and during emergencies with the help of on-demand translation services.

2. Use Visual Aids and Pictograms

Universal Symbols: Use pictograms and universal symbols that can be understood regardless of language. For example, a picture of a person running towards an exit can indicate evacuation, and a symbol of a fire can signal danger.

Illustrated Instructions: Create visual guides that use step-by-step images to demonstrate emergency procedures. This can help bridge language gaps and ensure that everyone understands what actions to take.

3. Leverage Technology

Translation Apps: Encourage the use of translation apps that can quickly translate spoken and written language. Apps like Google Translate can be useful in emergencies for real-time communication.

Automated Alerts: Use emergency alert systems that can automatically send messages in multiple languages. Some systems can detect the preferred language of the recipient based on their device settings and deliver alerts accordingly.

4. Community Engagement

Bilingual Volunteers: Recruit bilingual community members as volunteers to help disseminate information and provide assistance during emergencies. They can act as interpreters and help bridge the communication gap.

Cultural Sensitivity Training: Train emergency responders and volunteers in cultural sensitivity to better understand and communicate with non-native speakers. This can reduce misunderstandings and build trust.

5. Simplified Language

Plain Language Instructions: Use simple, direct language that is easy to understand, even for those with limited proficiency in the primary language.

Avoid jargon, technical terms, and complex sentences.

Repetition and Clarification: Repeat important messages and provide opportunities for individuals to ask questions or seek clarification. This helps ensure that everyone fully understands the information being communicated.

- **Communicating with Individuals with Disabilities**

1. Accessible Formats

Braille and Large Print: Ensure that written materials are available in accessible formats, such as braille for individuals who are blind and large print for those with low vision. This allows them to access critical information independently.

Audio Announcements: Provide audio versions of all written materials and instructions. For individuals who are blind or have low vision, audio announcements can be an essential tool for receiving timely information.

2. Sign Language and Captioning

Sign Language Interpreters: For individuals who are deaf or hard of hearing, ensure that sign language interpreters are available during emergency broadcasts and briefings. This can be done in person or through video remote interpreting services.

Captioning: All video content, including emergency broadcasts and instructional videos, should be captioned to make it accessible to those who are deaf or hard of hearing. Captioning ensures that these individuals can access the same information as everyone else.

3. Assistive Technologies

Text-to-Speech and Speech-to-Text Software: Encourage the use of assistive technologies such as text-to-speech and speech-to-text software. These tools can help individuals with disabilities access written information or communicate their needs effectively.

Hearing Loops and Amplifiers: In public spaces, such as emergency shelters, install hearing loops or provide personal amplifiers for those who are hard of hearing. These devices can help amplify sound and improve communication.

4. Simplified Communication Methods

Clear, Concise Instructions: When communicating with individuals with cognitive or intellectual disabilities, use clear and concise instructions. Break down complex information into simple steps, and avoid using abstract concepts.

Visual Supports: Use visual supports, such as pictures or symbols, to help individuals understand what is being communicated. Visual supports can enhance comprehension and provide a visual reference for what actions to take.

5. Pre-Planning and Drills

Emergency Drills: Conduct regular emergency drills that include individuals with disabilities. Practice not only the physical actions they need to take but also the communication methods that will be used during an emergency.

Personalized Emergency Plans: Work with individuals with disabilities to develop personalized emergency plans that take into account their specific needs and communication preferences. This can include designated helpers, specific routes, and accessible communication tools.

6. Training and Education

Disability Awareness Training: Provide disability awareness training to emergency responders, volunteers, and community members. This training should cover how to effectively communicate with individuals with various disabilities and understand their specific needs.

Empowerment and Self-Advocacy: Educate individuals with disabilities about their rights and how to advocate for themselves during emergencies. This includes understanding available resources and knowing how to request assistance.

- **Creating Inclusive Emergency Communication Plans**

1. Inclusive Alert Systems

Multi-Channel Alerts: Use a combination of communication channels, such as text messages, phone calls, emails, social media, and in-person announcements, to ensure that everyone receives the information. This is particularly important for reaching individuals with different disabilities or language needs.

Accessible Alert Features: Ensure that all alert systems are accessible to individuals with disabilities. This includes offering options for text-based alerts for those who are deaf or hard of hearing and voice alerts for those who are blind or have low vision.

2. Community Involvement

Engage with Disability Organizations: Collaborate with local organizations that serve individuals with disabilities to develop and refine emergency communication plans. These organizations can provide valuable insights into the needs of their clients and help ensure that communication strategies are effective and inclusive.

Feedback Mechanisms: Establish feedback mechanisms that allow individuals with disabilities and non-native speakers to provide input on emergency communication efforts. This feedback can help identify gaps and improve future responses.

3. Leverage Local Resources

Local Media: Partner with local media outlets that broadcast in multiple languages or provide accessible content. This can help ensure that emergency information reaches a wider audience.

Community Networks: Utilize existing community networks, such as neighborhood associations and faith-based organizations, to disseminate information and provide support to individuals with disabilities and language barriers.

4. Emergency Kits with Communication Tools

Personalized Emergency Kits: Encourage individuals with disabilities and non-native speakers to create personalized emergency kits that include communication tools such as communication boards, hearing aids, or translation devices. These kits should also contain written instructions in their preferred language or accessible format.

Effective communication during emergencies requires inclusive strategies that consider the diverse needs of all community members, especially those with language barriers and disabilities. By using multiple languages, visual aids, assistive technologies, and inclusive alert systems, we can ensure that everyone receives the critical information they need to stay safe. Preparing in advance, engaging with local resources, and empowering individuals to advocate for themselves are essential steps in overcoming communication barriers and creating a more resilient and inclusive community.

CHAPTER 8

Practice Makes Perfect: Drills and Simulations

Planning and Conducting Communication Drills

Practicing communication during emergencies is one of the most critical steps in preparing for real-life disaster scenarios. Communication drills ensure that everyone knows how to relay and receive important information, respond appropriately, and stay connected when it matters most. This is especially important for families, organizations, and communities because emergencies can create confusion, and clear communication is essential for coordinating responses and keeping everyone safe. To make sure communication runs smoothly, it's important to plan and conduct regular drills.

- **Understanding the Importance of Communication Drills**

Effective communication is the backbone of a well-coordinated emergency response. It ensures that individuals, teams, and communities can quickly share updates, report dangers, and provide instructions. However, even with the best communication systems in place, they can be useless if people don't know how to use them during emergencies. This is where communication drills come in. Drills are like rehearsals for real-life events. They allow people to practice under simulated conditions, helping them understand how the communication systems work and what protocols to follow.

Drills also help identify gaps in the communication system, such as equipment malfunctions, unclear messaging, or individuals who may need more training. When issues are identified, adjustments can be made to improve overall preparedness. For these reasons, communication drills should be conducted regularly, ensuring that everyone involved remains familiar with the processes and systems.

• Steps for Planning Communication Drills

1. Define the Objectives

Before conducting any drill, it's crucial to have clear objectives. Objectives help focus the drill on specific areas of improvement. Ask yourself, what are you trying to achieve with the drill? Objectives could include testing the effectiveness of your emergency communication equipment, ensuring that participants know how to contact key personnel, or making sure everyone can follow and give instructions clearly under pressure. Once objectives are defined, the entire drill can be designed to meet those goals.

2. Develop a Communication Plan

A communication plan outlines how information will flow during emergencies. It specifies who communicates with whom, through which channels, and using what methods. This plan should be as detailed as possible, covering different types of emergencies and communication tools like radios, phones, text alerts, or social media. When planning the drill, ensure that everyone knows the communication plan and is ready to implement it during the exercise.

3. Set Up Realistic Scenarios

The more realistic the drill, the better the participants will be able to prepare for a real-life situation. Create scenarios that mimic potential emergencies. These could include natural disasters like floods, hurricanes, or fires, or man-made events like power outages or communication system failures. The scenarios should challenge the communication systems and force participants to rely on their training to stay connected. Include potential disruptions, like power loss or network failures, to simulate real-world obstacles.

4. Assign Roles and Responsibilities

During any emergency, different people will have different roles to play. Assign roles to participants during the drill. Some participants may be in charge of relaying emergency alerts, while others may need to coordinate evacuation or provide critical updates to others. Everyone should know their role in the communication chain and be prepared to act accordingly. Be sure to include people of all ages and abilities, including children and those with disabilities, to practice inclusive communication methods.

5. Prepare Communication Tools and Equipment

Before the drill begins, ensure all communication tools and equipment are in working order. This could include radios, satellite phones, walkie-talkies, smartphones, and other devices used in the communication plan. It's also important to have backup power sources available, such as batteries or generators, in case of power failure. Part of the drill should test whether all of these tools are working properly and whether participants can use them effectively.

- **Conducting the Communication Drill**

1. Start with a Briefing

Before the drill begins, gather all participants for a briefing. Explain the scenario they are about to encounter, but do not reveal every detail. For instance, if the drill is based on a sudden weather emergency, explain that they will need to rely on their communication tools to stay informed and follow emergency instructions. The briefing helps everyone understand what's expected and ensures they are mentally prepared to engage in the exercise.

2. Simulate the Emergency

Once the drill begins, introduce the emergency scenario. This could be done through alarms, simulated news broadcasts, or messages indicating that a disaster is happening. Participants should immediately begin using the communication methods outlined in the communication plan to share information, report issues, and respond to the situation. Everyone should follow the same protocols they would during a real emergency.

3. Observe and Take Notes

As the drill progresses, it's important to observe how well participants communicate. Pay attention to how quickly information is relayed, whether any equipment malfunctions, and how well participants understand and follow instructions. Taking notes during the drill helps identify areas where communication may break down or where additional training may be needed. Observers should also monitor whether any communication tools or protocols are too complicated, causing confusion or delays.

4. Challenge the Participants

Introduce unexpected elements to make the drill more realistic. For example, if the scenario is a natural disaster, simulate a power outage that forces participants to switch to backup communication systems. Or introduce a scenario where key personnel are unavailable, requiring participants to adapt and figure out alternate ways to communicate. Challenging the participants ensures they are not just going through the motions but thinking critically about how to maintain effective communication during chaos.

5. Debrief and Analyze the Results

Once the drill is over, conduct a debriefing session. Gather all participants and review what went well and what didn't. Allow everyone to share their experiences, concerns, and suggestions for improvement. Analyzing the results helps identify any weaknesses in the communication system. Perhaps some communication tools were not used correctly, or certain protocols were too slow. Whatever the case, the debriefing provides an opportunity to refine the emergency communication plan.

- **Improving Future Drills**

After conducting a drill, it's important to make necessary improvements. Based on the debriefing feedback, update your communication plan to address any issues identified during the exercise. This might mean changing the way certain information is relayed, adding more training for certain roles, or adjusting the communication tools used. The goal is to continuously improve communication strategies and prepare for any future emergencies.

To make future drills even more effective:
- Rotate roles so that everyone gets the opportunity to practice different communication responsibilities.
- Conduct drills at different times of the day or in different weather conditions to simulate more varied emergency scenarios.
- Involve other members of the community, such as local emergency responders, to make the drill more realistic and comprehensive.

- Repeat drills regularly to ensure that skills and knowledge remain fresh, especially for new participants or after any significant changes to the communication plan.

Inclusive Drills for All Ages and Abilities

It's important to ensure that communication drills are inclusive. This means considering the needs of children, elderly individuals, and people with disabilities. For example, children should be taught how to respond to emergencies in a way that is appropriate for their age, while individuals with hearing or visual impairments may need alternative communication tools, such as sign language interpreters or text-based alerts. Ensuring that everyone can participate fully in drills guarantees that no one is left behind during a real emergency.

Communication drills are essential for preparing individuals, families, and communities for emergencies. By planning realistic scenarios, using appropriate communication tools, assigning clear roles, and challenging participants, drills can help everyone stay connected when it matters most. Regular practice, observation, and improvement ensure that communication systems function effectively during a real emergency, keeping people informed, safe, and ready to respond.

Evaluating and Improving Your Communication Plan

A well-crafted communication plan is essential for responding effectively to emergencies, but it's not enough to just create the plan—you also need to regularly evaluate and improve it. Evaluating a communication plan helps identify strengths and weaknesses, ensuring that everyone can stay informed and connected when it matters most. Through assessments, reviews, and drills, the communication plan can be fine-tuned for greater clarity, efficiency, and reliability.

- **Why Evaluation is Important**

A communication plan outlines how information should flow in the event of an emergency, who should be contacted, and which tools should be used. However, emergencies are unpredictable, and what works well in theory may not work in practice. By evaluating the communication plan, you can determine how effectively it functions during real or simulated emergencies.

Evaluating the plan helps uncover hidden issues such as unclear instructions, faulty equipment, or protocols that are too complicated to follow. By identifying and addressing these problems early on, you improve the plan's efficiency and increase the likelihood of successful communication during a real disaster. Without regular evaluations, gaps in the communication process may go unnoticed until it's too late.

- **Assessing Key Components of Your Plan**

The first step in evaluating a communication plan is to assess its key components. This involves reviewing the plan's structure, procedures, and tools to ensure they meet the needs of everyone involved. There are several elements to focus on when evaluating the communication plan:

Clarity of Roles and Responsibilities: It's important that everyone understands their role in the communication process. Is it clear who is responsible for contacting whom in an emergency? Does everyone know what their communication responsibilities are, and do they have the right tools to carry out their role?

Effectiveness of Communication Channels: The methods used for communication, such as radios, phones, and social media, should be evaluated for reliability and ease of use. Are the channels appropriate for the type of emergency? Do they function correctly under stress or technical challenges?

Backup Systems: Emergencies can disrupt primary communication channels. Evaluating whether backup systems (like satellite phones or walkie-talkies) are properly in place and accessible is critical. Do people know how to use backup devices in case the primary system fails?

Timeliness of Communication: In emergencies, the speed of communication is crucial. Evaluating how quickly messages are sent, received, and understood will help determine if the plan allows for timely information sharing. Delays can cause confusion or put people at risk.

Inclusivity and Accessibility: The communication plan should account for the needs of all participants, including children, the elderly, and people with disabilities. Evaluate whether the plan provides adequate accommodations for these individuals, such as visual or hearing aids, alternative communication methods, or age-appropriate instructions.

- **Conducting Communication Drills**

Drills are one of the most effective ways to evaluate a communication plan. They allow you to simulate emergency situations and test the plan under realistic conditions. Drills can range from small exercises focused on specific communication tools to full-scale drills involving multiple parties.

When conducting drills, it's essential to simulate different types of emergencies. For instance, a power outage drill will test backup communication methods, while a weather-related scenario may evaluate how well the communication plan handles widespread emergencies. By varying the drill scenarios, you can identify different weaknesses in the communication plan and make more informed adjustments.

During the drill, assess the following:

- How quickly participants respond to the emergency scenario.
- How effectively information is shared across the communication chain.
- Whether all participants can follow instructions clearly and easily.
- Any technical issues that arise with communication devices or systems.

These observations provide valuable data on how well the communication plan functions under pressure.

Gathering Feedback from Participants

After conducting a drill, it's important to gather feedback from everyone involved. Participants' firsthand experiences are invaluable in identifying problems that may not be obvious from an outside perspective. They can provide insights into issues such as:

- Confusing instructions or unclear roles.

- Tools or systems that were difficult to use.
- Delays or bottlenecks in communication.

Encourage participants to share both positive and negative feedback, as well as any suggestions for improvement. This can be done through a debriefing session immediately after the drill, where everyone has the opportunity to discuss what worked well and what didn't. Alternatively, written feedback forms or surveys can be distributed for more detailed responses.

Analyzing the Results

Once feedback has been gathered, it's time to analyze the results of the drill. Look for patterns in the feedback to identify common areas of concern. For example, if multiple participants reported confusion over a particular procedure, this may indicate a need for clearer instructions or additional training.

In addition to reviewing feedback, examine the data from the drill itself. Were there any major delays in communication? Did the backup systems function as expected? Were all participants able to stay in contact throughout the drill? Use this information to pinpoint specific problems that need to be addressed.

- **Making Necessary Adjustments**

After analyzing the drill results and participant feedback, you can begin making improvements to the communication plan. This may involve updating certain procedures, retraining individuals on their roles, or replacing outdated or faulty equipment. Here are some common areas where adjustments may be necessary:

Simplifying Procedures: If the drill revealed that some steps were too complicated or caused delays, simplify the procedures to make them easier to follow.

Upgrading Communication Tools: If certain devices or systems failed during the drill, it may be time to upgrade to more reliable equipment or add backup options.

Improving Clarity: If participants found certain instructions unclear, update the language to make it more straightforward and easy to understand. Visual aids like diagrams or flowcharts can help clarify complex procedures.

Strengthening Backup Systems: Ensure that backup communication methods are fully functional and that all participants are trained on how to use them in case the primary system fails.

- **Reviewing and Refining Regularly**

Improving a communication plan is not a one-time process. Regular reviews and updates are necessary to keep the plan effective as new technologies emerge, team members change, or new threats arise. Set a schedule for reviewing the communication plan at least once a year, or more frequently if circumstances change. For example, after a natural disaster or other real-life emergency, the communication plan should be revisited to address any shortcomings that were encountered.

Also, continue conducting drills on a regular basis to reinforce communication practices and ensure that everyone remains familiar with the plan. As you conduct more drills and gather additional feedback, the communication plan will evolve and improve over time, ensuring it stays robust and reliable.

Training and Education

An essential part of improving the communication plan is ongoing training for all participants. Regular education sessions on using communication tools, following protocols, and responding to emergencies help ensure that everyone is prepared when an actual disaster strikes. Training should be tailored to the needs of different participants, including special training for vulnerable populations like children or individuals with disabilities. By keeping everyone well-informed and practiced, the communication plan will be more effective in the long run.

Evaluating and improving your communication plan is a continuous process that involves careful assessment, regular practice, and constant refinement. By conducting drills, gathering feedback, analyzing results, and making necessary adjustments, you can ensure that your communication plan remains effective and reliable in the face of any emergency. Regular evaluation helps close gaps, strengthens communication channels, and keeps everyone prepared, ensuring safety and coordination when it's needed most.

Involving Community and Neighbors in Drills

Involving your community and neighbors in emergency communication drills offers numerous benefits, creating a stronger, more cohesive response to disasters. When emergencies happen, having a network of support can make a significant difference in how quickly and efficiently everyone can respond. By including those around you in practice drills, you're not only building a system of mutual aid but also improving the overall preparedness of your entire community.

Building Trust and Cooperation

One of the biggest advantages of involving your neighbors in emergency drills is the development of trust and cooperation. In times of crisis, it's important to know you can rely on the people nearby. By practicing together, neighbors become more familiar with each other, learn to work as a team, and understand each person's strengths. When the real emergency happens, this trust ensures that everyone can coordinate efforts more smoothly and help each other more effectively.

Trust is also critical for communication. If people know and trust each other, they are more likely to share information and provide assistance in a timely manner. Neighbors who have participated in drills together will know who has specialized skills, like first aid training or access to equipment like generators, and who may need extra help during an emergency.

Fostering a Sense of Community

Including neighbors in emergency drills fosters a strong sense of community, which is crucial for disaster preparedness. In many neighborhoods, people may not interact much on a daily basis. However, organizing drills encourages residents to come together for a common goal. These activities provide an opportunity to build relationships that could prove life-saving during an emergency.

A sense of community also brings comfort and reassurance during stressful times. When everyone knows that they're part of a supportive group, it helps reduce panic and fear in the face of an emergency. This shared responsibility encourages people to check on each other and offer assistance to those who may be more vulnerable.

Creating a Local Network of Support

Emergencies often disrupt communication systems, making it difficult to reach authorities or get help from far away. Involving neighbors in communication drills allows you to create a local network of support. This network ensures that even if external help is delayed, people within the community can assist one another and share crucial information.

This local network could include:
- A group text or messaging app to quickly alert neighbors of an emergency.
- A plan for checking in on vulnerable residents, such as the elderly or people with disabilities.
- A list of local resources, such as who has extra food, water, or first aid supplies.

By building this network through regular drills, the community becomes better equipped to handle challenges independently, without relying solely on outside aid.

Improving Communication Channels

Effective communication is vital during emergencies. Drills that involve the community help ensure that everyone knows how to communicate clearly and efficiently. By practicing different methods of communication, such as using radios, cell phones, or even face-to-face contact, neighbors can establish reliable channels for sharing information.

During drills, you can test various communication tools to see what works best in your specific area. For example, you might find that walkie-talkies work well in your neighborhood when cell phone towers are down, or that setting up a central meeting point is a good way to distribute information in person. Practicing with these tools ensures that everyone knows how to use them and when to switch to a backup method if needed.

Helping Vulnerable Populations

Communities often include individuals who may be more vulnerable during emergencies, such as children, the elderly, or people with disabilities. Including neighbors in drills helps ensure that everyone is aware of the special needs of these individuals and can plan accordingly.

By identifying and addressing these needs during a drill, you can create a plan for providing assistance. This might involve assigning specific neighbors to check on vulnerable individuals or developing alternative communication methods for those who may struggle with standard systems. Working together as a community ensures that no one is left behind and that the needs of all residents are considered and met.

Gaining New Skills and Knowledge

Involving the community in drills allows everyone to gain new skills and knowledge that can be beneficial in an emergency. For example, during a drill, neighbors might learn how to operate communication equipment they aren't familiar with, such as a ham radio or satellite phone. Others might learn basic first aid or survival skills, which can be invaluable during a disaster.

These shared learning experiences benefit the entire community. The more skills and knowledge that are spread throughout the neighborhood, the better equipped everyone will be to respond effectively. Additionally, these drills give people a chance to practice skills in a low-pressure environment, so they're more confident and prepared when an actual emergency occurs.

Strengthening Problem-solving Abilities

Drills provide an opportunity for neighbors to work through potential problems together. By practicing in a simulated emergency scenario, the community can identify weak points in the plan or unexpected challenges that need to be addressed. For instance, during a drill, neighbors may realize that certain areas of the neighborhood have poor communication coverage, or that some residents don't have access to emergency supplies.

By working together to solve these problems in advance, the community becomes better prepared to handle real-life emergencies. Problem-solving as a group also helps residents think critically and remain calm under pressure, which is essential during an actual crisis.

Sharing Resources and Tools

During an emergency, resources like food, water, and communication equipment can become limited. By including neighbors in drills, communities can develop a plan for sharing resources more efficiently. Drills allow neighbors to take stock of what equipment and supplies are available and how they can be distributed in an emergency.

For example, one neighbor might have a generator, while another has a large water supply. By practicing how these resources will be shared or accessed, the community can ensure that everyone has what they need to survive. This cooperation can prevent panic and ensure that resources are used wisely and effectively.

Encouraging Responsibility and Preparedness

Participating in drills encourages individuals to take personal responsibility for their preparedness. When neighbors see others actively participating in emergency planning, it creates a culture of preparedness throughout the community. People are more likely to stock up on supplies, keep their communication devices charged, and stay informed about potential risks when they know they're part of a larger effort.

This sense of responsibility extends to making sure others in the community are also prepared. Neighbors may check in on each other's readiness or offer to help those who are struggling to gather supplies or equipment. This shared commitment to preparedness strengthens the entire community.

Boosting Morale and Confidence

Lastly, involving the community in drills boosts morale and gives everyone more confidence in their ability to handle emergencies. By practicing together, neighbors can see firsthand that they are capable of responding effectively, even in difficult situations. This increased confidence reduces fear and anxiety, making it easier to remain calm and focused during an actual emergency.

Additionally, knowing that the entire community is working together to stay prepared creates a sense of solidarity and shared purpose. When people feel connected to their neighbors and know they can rely on one another, they're more likely to feel empowered rather than helpless in the face of disaster.

Involving the community and neighbors in emergency communication drills is a powerful way to build a network of support, improve communication systems, and ensure that everyone is prepared for whatever challenges may arise. Through cooperation, trust, and shared responsibility, the entire community becomes stronger and better equipped to handle emergencies.

CHAPTER 9

Advanced Communication Techniques for Preppers

Mesh Networks and Off-Grid Internet

Mesh networks are an innovative and effective way to communicate during emergencies, especially when traditional internet and phone services are unavailable. These networks create a web of connected devices, allowing communication without relying on centralized infrastructure like cell towers or internet service providers. Understanding how mesh networks work and how they can be applied for off-grid communication is crucial for anyone preparing for a disaster scenario.

- What is a Mesh Network?

A mesh network is a decentralized system where devices, known as nodes, connect directly to each other. Unlike traditional networks that rely on a central hub (like a router or cell tower), mesh networks allow each device to communicate with others within range. The network grows stronger and more reliable as more devices are added. If one node fails or goes offline, the system reroutes data through other nearby nodes, ensuring that communication can continue even if some parts of the network are disrupted.

In a typical mesh network, devices such as smartphones, computers, or specialized mesh network devices (like routers or radios) act as both transmitters and receivers. These devices pass information along the network, enabling messages to reach distant nodes by hopping from one device to another. This self-healing ability makes mesh networks particularly resilient, which is ideal for emergency situations.

How Mesh Networks Work in Emergencies

During disasters, regular communication channels often fail due to infrastructure damage or power outages. Mesh networks shine in these situations because they don't rely on centralized systems that can easily break down. As long as there are enough active nodes within range of each other, communication can continue across the network.

In an emergency scenario, each person in a community could have a device that connects to the mesh network. For instance, smartphones equipped with mesh networking apps or small portable routers can communicate with each other even when there's no internet or cellular service. This means messages, alerts, and critical information can still be passed along within the community.

Mesh networks are also useful for connecting first responders with civilians in an emergency. If traditional radio or phone lines are down, mesh-enabled devices can be used to coordinate rescue operations, share vital updates, and ensure that everyone remains connected.

Building and Expanding a Mesh Network

Setting up a mesh network for emergency communication requires a few key components. Devices like smartphones, laptops, or dedicated mesh routers can be equipped with the necessary software to participate in a mesh network. Apps like FireChat, Bridgefy, and Serval Mesh enable phones to communicate with each other directly without requiring an internet connection. These apps use Bluetooth or Wi-Fi to form a mesh network with nearby devices.

To create a more robust and far-reaching network, dedicated mesh routers or radios can be used. These devices are specifically designed to create large mesh networks, making them ideal for use in neighborhoods, communities, or even larger areas. Mesh routers, like those made by companies such as GoTenna or Ubiquiti, can extend the range of the network, allowing communication over greater distances. These routers are portable and can run on battery or solar power, making them suitable for off-grid use.

Expanding the mesh network depends on the number of participants and the range of their devices. The more people who have mesh-enabled devices, the larger and more reliable the network becomes. For instance, in a community where many residents have mesh-capable routers, the network can cover a wide area, ensuring that communication remains possible even across long distances.

Off-Grid Internet with Mesh Networks

Mesh networks not only allow for local communication; they can also provide access to the internet in off-grid situations. While the network itself doesn't require the internet to function, it can connect to the internet if at least one node has access to a working internet connection. This node acts as a gateway, allowing other devices in the network to share the connection.

For example, if someone in a mesh network has a satellite internet connection or a working mobile hotspot, they can provide internet access to the entire network. The connection will be distributed across all the nodes, ensuring that everyone on the network can access important online information, news updates, or emergency services.

In disaster situations where power outages and infrastructure damage make it difficult to access the internet, this off-grid capability becomes especially valuable. Mesh networks can keep a community connected to the outside world, even when traditional internet service is down.

Advantages of Mesh Networks in Emergency Preparedness

Mesh networks offer several significant advantages for preppers and those concerned with emergency preparedness. One of the most important is their ability to function without relying on any centralized infrastructure. When phone lines, internet services, or power grids fail, a mesh network can keep people connected, ensuring that critical information and resources can still be shared.

Another key benefit is the resilience of the network. Since each device or node in a mesh network is capable of passing along information, the network can adapt to changes or disruptions. If one node goes offline, the system automatically reroutes data through other nearby nodes. This self-healing capability ensures that the network remains functional even when parts of it are damaged.

Mesh networks also provide greater privacy and security. Since they operate independently of centralized systems, they can be more difficult for outsiders to monitor or disrupt. This is particularly important in emergencies, where maintaining secure communication is crucial. While the basic mesh network is not inherently encrypted, many mesh-enabled apps and devices offer encryption options, ensuring that sensitive information remains protected.

Challenges and Limitations of Mesh Networks

While mesh networks are a powerful tool for emergency communication, they are not without their challenges. One limitation is range. The strength and coverage of a mesh network depend on the number and placement of nodes. If there are too few devices in a given area, the network may not be able to reach all users. In rural or sparsely populated areas, setting up a reliable mesh network may require additional equipment, such as long-range routers or repeaters.

Another challenge is bandwidth. As data is passed from one node to another, the speed and quality of the connection can degrade, especially if the network is overloaded with too much traffic. This means that while mesh networks are great for sending text messages or basic updates, they may struggle with bandwidth-heavy tasks like video streaming or large file transfers.

Lastly, mesh networks require participation. For the network to be effective, enough people must have mesh-enabled devices or routers. Encouraging your community to invest in and set up these devices is important for building a strong and reliable mesh network.

Mesh networks offer a flexible, resilient, and decentralized way to maintain communication during emergencies. By using a web of connected devices, these networks can function without relying on traditional infrastructure, making them ideal for off-grid communication in disaster scenarios. For preppers, setting up a mesh network in advance ensures that even when the internet and phone lines go down, essential communication can continue. Though mesh networks come with challenges like range and bandwidth limitations, their advantages in emergency preparedness make them a valuable tool for staying connected and informed.

Encrypted Communications for Privacy and Security

During disasters, communication plays a crucial role in ensuring the safety and coordination of people, families, and communities. However, this communication must also be secure. In a crisis, sensitive information like personal details, medical emergencies, and safety plans can be highly valuable. Ensuring that this information stays private and protected from malicious individuals is why encrypted communication is so important.

Encryption refers to the process of converting information into a code that can only be decoded or understood by those who have the right key or password. When communication is encrypted, it prevents unauthorized people from accessing or reading it. In an emergency, encrypted communication can help protect your privacy and safeguard your information from hackers, thieves, or others who might want to exploit vulnerable situations.

Why Encryption is Important in Emergencies

During disasters, such as natural calamities or societal disruptions, communication systems may be compromised or weakened. In these situations, many people turn to alternative communication methods like radios, smartphones, or online platforms to stay in touch. However, these platforms are not always secure, making them potential targets for hackers who could intercept messages, steal personal data, or even spread false information.

Encryption protects the privacy of your conversations, keeping them out of the hands of those who might misuse them. In a crisis, this is especially important because criminals might try to take advantage of the chaos to exploit people. For example, they might attempt to steal your financial information or find out where you are hiding valuable supplies. By using encryption, you ensure that even if someone tries to access your messages, they won't be able to understand them without the right decryption key.

Encryption is also important for securing sensitive information like medical details or safety plans. If you're organizing a group effort to evacuate or gather supplies, you wouldn't want someone outside your trusted group to know your exact movements or locations. Encryption helps ensure that only the intended recipients of your messages can access this critical information.

How Encryption Works

Encryption involves scrambling data into a form that cannot be easily understood. This process uses algorithms to change the content of a message so that it becomes unreadable. To access the original message, the recipient needs a decryption key, which allows them to unlock and decode the scrambled data.

There are two main types of encryption: symmetric and asymmetric. In symmetric encryption, both the sender and recipient use the same key to encrypt and decrypt messages. This method is fast and efficient but requires that both parties share the same secret key, which can be difficult in an emergency situation.

Asymmetric encryption, on the other hand, uses two different keys—a public key and a private key. The public key is used to encrypt the message, while the private key is used to decrypt it. Only the person with the private key can access the original message, making this method more secure but also slightly slower than symmetric encryption.

Modern communication apps and platforms often use a combination of these encryption methods to secure messages. For instance, apps like Signal and WhatsApp offer end-to-end encryption, which means that only the sender and receiver of the message can read it, and even the company providing the app can't access the message content.

Choosing Encrypted Communication Tools

There are many tools and platforms that offer encrypted communication, but not all are created equal. It's important to choose communication tools that provide strong encryption, are easy to use, and work well in emergency situations. Here are a few options:

Messaging Apps: Apps like Signal, WhatsApp, and Telegram offer end-to-end encryption, ensuring that only the intended recipient can read your messages. Signal is often regarded as one of the most secure messaging apps because it is open source, meaning its code is publicly available for review, and it does not store user data on its servers.

Email Encryption: Regular email services are not encrypted by default, but using tools like ProtonMail or encrypted email services with PGP (Pretty Good Privacy) can ensure that your email communications are secure.

Encrypted Radios: Some two-way radios offer encryption options, ensuring that your conversations over the radio cannot be easily intercepted by unauthorized listeners. This can be especially useful in prepping scenarios where radios are commonly used for communication.

VPNs (Virtual Private Networks): VPNs create a secure, encrypted tunnel for your internet connection, preventing hackers from monitoring or tampering with your online activity. During emergencies, when using public or unsecured networks might be necessary, VPNs offer an additional layer of protection.

Secure File Sharing: If you need to share important documents, photos, or other files, make sure to use a service that provides encrypted file transfers. Tools like Tresorit and SpiderOak offer encrypted cloud storage and file sharing, ensuring that only authorized users can access the content.

- **Maintaining Security During a Crisis**

Encryption is one part of a larger strategy for keeping your communications secure. Here are some additional steps to take during emergencies to enhance privacy and security:

Use Strong Passwords: Ensure that all your communication apps, devices, and accounts are protected by strong, unique passwords. Avoid using easily guessable information like birthdays or names, and consider using a password manager to keep track of your passwords securely.

Update Your Software: Outdated software can have vulnerabilities that hackers can exploit. Regularly updating your devices and apps ensures that you have the latest security patches and are protected against known threats.

Limit the Information You Share: Even with encryption, it's important to be mindful of what information you're sharing. Avoid broadcasting your exact location, detailed plans, or other sensitive information unless absolutely necessary.

Be Wary of Phishing: During emergencies, cybercriminals may try to exploit fear and confusion by sending fake alerts, emails, or messages that appear to come from trusted sources. Always double-check the sender and be cautious about clicking on unfamiliar links or providing personal information.

Verify Identities: When communicating with others, especially during a crisis, it's important to verify that the person you're speaking to is who they claim to be. Hackers can sometimes impersonate trusted contacts in an attempt to gain access to sensitive information.

- **Challenges of Encrypted Communication**

While encryption offers robust security, it's not without challenges. One issue is that not all devices and platforms support encryption, which can limit your communication options. Additionally, encryption can sometimes slow down communication, as it requires additional processing to encode and decode messages. In fast-moving disaster scenarios, this delay could potentially be an inconvenience.

Another challenge is that encryption only protects the content of your messages, not the metadata. Metadata includes information like the time the message was sent, who the sender and receiver are, and other details that could still reveal valuable information. To fully protect your privacy, it's important to use tools that minimize the amount of metadata they collect.

Encrypted communication is an essential tool for ensuring privacy and security during disasters. By encrypting your messages and using secure platforms, you can protect yourself from hackers, criminals, and others who might seek to exploit the situation. While encryption has its challenges, it remains one of the best ways to keep sensitive information safe and maintain clear, secure communication when it matters most. Taking the time to set up encrypted communication tools before an emergency can make a significant difference in your ability to stay connected and protected during a crisis.

Utilizing Morse Code and Other Non-Verbal Communication Methods

Morse code and other non-verbal communication methods have been used for centuries as reliable ways to send messages when more common methods are unavailable. These techniques are simple yet powerful tools, particularly in situations where radios, phones, or other devices are not working. Knowing how to communicate using Morse code, hand signals, or visual cues can be a lifesaver in emergency scenarios where conventional communication is compromised.

Morse code is one of the most well-known non-verbal communication methods. Developed in the early 19th century by Samuel Morse, it uses a series of dots (short signals) and dashes (long signals) to represent letters, numbers, and punctuation. Each letter or number in the alphabet is given its own unique combination of dots and dashes. For instance, the letter "A" is represented by a dot followed by a dash (· —), while the letter "B" is dash followed by three dots (— · · ·). This makes Morse code a highly flexible and universal language for transmitting messages.

One of the biggest advantages of Morse code is that it can be communicated in various ways, including sound, light, and even touch. For example, Morse code can be transmitted through tapping, with short taps representing dots and longer taps representing dashes. It can also be sent using a flashlight by flashing short and long bursts of light, or through audio signals like beeping sounds. This flexibility makes Morse code especially useful in emergencies when traditional communication devices might not be available or functioning.

To use Morse code effectively, it's important to familiarize yourself with the basic alphabet and practice sending and receiving simple messages. Many preppers keep a printed Morse code chart handy so they can quickly look up letters or numbers in an emergency. There are also smartphone apps that can translate typed text into Morse code or vice versa, making it easier for beginners to get started. However, it's still important to know how to send Morse code manually in case technology fails.

Another key feature of Morse code is the SOS signal. SOS (· · · — — — · · ·) is an internationally recognized distress signal that can be sent in Morse code to alert others that you need help. It's easy to remember and can be transmitted through a variety of mediums, making it an essential tool for any prepper or emergency responder. Whether you're stranded in a remote area or facing a natural disaster, knowing how to send an SOS signal in Morse code can help you get assistance quickly.

In addition to Morse code, there are other non-verbal communication methods that can be useful in emergency situations. Hand signals, for example, are commonly used in environments where speaking out loud might not be possible or safe, such as in noisy areas or when stealth is required. Many organizations, including military forces and outdoor survival groups, use a set of standard hand signals to convey important messages. These signals might include raising a hand to signal "stop," pointing in a certain direction to indicate movement, or holding up a specific number of fingers to communicate numbers.

Hand signals can be used effectively for communication within a small group, especially if everyone understands the same set of signals. It's important to practice using hand signals with family members or group members so that everyone knows what each signal means. This practice ensures that communication can happen smoothly even when speech is not an option. Hand signals are particularly helpful in low-visibility situations, such as during heavy rain, fog, or at night when verbal communication may be difficult.

Visual signals are another non-verbal communication method that can be used over longer distances. These signals can include anything from waving a brightly colored flag or cloth to creating smoke signals. In some cases, even a mirror can be used to reflect sunlight and send flashes of light to someone far away. This technique, known as "heliography," has been used historically for long-distance communication, particularly in open areas like deserts or at sea.

Smoke signals are one of the oldest forms of long-distance visual communication. They were used by Indigenous peoples and other cultures around the world to send messages across large areas. By creating a fire and using a blanket or other material to block and release smoke in puffs, different patterns can be created to communicate specific messages. While smoke signals are less common today, they can still be useful in certain survival situations, especially if you're in a remote area and need to signal for help.

Flag signaling, also known as semaphore, is another form of non-verbal communication that involves using flags to send messages. Semaphore uses a combination of arm and flag positions to represent different letters or numbers, much like Morse code. This method was historically used by ships to communicate over long distances, and it can still be a valuable tool in areas where visual communication is necessary. While semaphore requires practice to learn the different positions for each letter, it can be a fun and useful skill to master, especially for groups working together in a large outdoor area.

Whistling is another effective way to communicate over long distances, especially in outdoor environments. Different whistle patterns can be used to send simple messages, such as a series of short whistles to call attention or a long whistle to signal danger. In some cultures, whistled languages have been developed to communicate complex ideas across great distances. For example, the whistled language of the Canary Islands, known as "Silbo Gomero," allows speakers to communicate across deep valleys and is still in use today.

In survival situations, body language also plays a crucial role in non-verbal communication. Simple gestures like nodding or shaking your head, pointing, or using facial expressions can convey important information without the need for words. Understanding and interpreting body language can help you communicate effectively with others, especially if there is a language barrier or if someone is unable to speak due to injury or shock.

Flags, lights, and mirrors can also be used to communicate over large distances. For example, in maritime or military situations, signal flags are used to send messages between ships or between ships and shore. Similarly, mirrors or other reflective surfaces can be used to flash signals over long distances during daylight hours. These flashes can be coded using patterns similar to Morse code, allowing for a variety of messages to be transmitted even when no electronic communication devices are available.

In summary, Morse code and other non-verbal communication methods are invaluable tools for preppers and anyone facing an emergency situation. By learning how to use Morse code, hand signals, visual cues, and other non-verbal methods, you can ensure that you have multiple ways to communicate even when traditional methods fail. These skills are simple to learn, but they require practice and preparation to use effectively. Having these tools in your communication toolkit will help you stay connected, safe, and informed in any emergency scenario.

CHAPTER 10

Real-Life Case Studies and Lessons Learned

Success Stories of Effective Emergency Communication

Effective emergency communication can make the difference between life and death in critical situations. Throughout history, there have been numerous instances where clear, timely communication saved lives, prevented disasters, and ensured safety. These real-life success stories demonstrate the importance of having well-planned communication strategies in place.

One notable example comes from the 2010 earthquake in Haiti. This catastrophic event left the country in chaos, with communication systems severely damaged. However, one of the factors that helped save thousands of lives was the use of mobile technology and social media platforms like Twitter. The international community, along with local Haitians, used these tools to send and receive critical information about where help was needed. Organizations like the Red Cross partnered with tech companies to set up SMS systems that allowed people to report their locations and request assistance. This quick response through mobile communication helped rescue teams reach those trapped under rubble and distribute aid more efficiently.

Another case of successful emergency communication occurred during Hurricane Sandy in 2012, which hit the East Coast of the United States. As the hurricane approached, local, state, and federal agencies worked together to broadcast real-time alerts through various channels, including TV, radio, social media, and emergency text alerts. The National Oceanic and Atmospheric Administration (NOAA) played a key role in providing accurate weather forecasts and storm tracking. In New York City, Mayor Bloomberg's office set up regular press briefings to update the public on safety measures, evacuation routes, and emergency shelters. The widespread use of communication tools helped ensure that people in the storm's path were well-informed and able to evacuate in time, reducing the loss of life.

The 2018 Camp Fire in California, one of the deadliest wildfires in the state's history, also highlights the importance of clear communication during disasters. Emergency services, including the California Department of Forestry and Fire Protection (CAL FIRE), used both traditional and modern communication methods to keep residents informed. They sent out automated phone calls, emergency alerts via text, and updates through social media platforms to warn people about the approaching fire. Local radio stations also played a critical role in keeping residents informed. The use of these diverse communication channels allowed many to evacuate safely before the fire reached their communities.

Another successful communication effort took place during the 2004 Indian Ocean tsunami. In this disaster, an earthquake triggered a massive tsunami that affected several countries, including Indonesia, Thailand, Sri Lanka, and India. Despite the devastation, some areas managed to reduce the loss of life due to early warning systems. In Thailand, local communities had been trained to recognize natural signs of a tsunami, such as receding water along the coast. When these signs were observed, local authorities and community members quickly alerted others, leading to timely evacuations. In some parts of India and Sri Lanka, traditional methods like drum beating and using loudspeakers were employed to warn villagers about the incoming waves. These simple yet effective communication methods helped save many lives.

The 2011 Tohoku earthquake and tsunami in Japan also showcased the critical role of effective communication. Japan's advanced early warning systems sent out alerts via television, radio, and cell phones seconds after the earthquake was detected. These alerts gave people a brief but crucial window of time to prepare for the earthquake and the subsequent tsunami. The Japanese government also used real-time communication to update the public on safety measures, evacuation orders, and emergency resources. Despite the immense destruction, the swift communication response helped save countless lives and prevent even greater loss.

During the COVID-19 pandemic, communication played an essential role in public health and safety. Governments and health organizations around the world used various channels to disseminate information about the virus, safety protocols, and vaccination efforts. Social media, public service announcements, and press briefings were key tools in informing the public about mask-wearing, social distancing, and hygiene measures. One notable success story came from New Zealand, where the government's clear and consistent communication strategy, led by Prime Minister Jacinda Ardern, helped keep the virus under control. Regular updates, clear guidelines, and transparent messaging reassured the public and encouraged compliance with health measures.

In another instance, during the 2010 Chilean mine rescue, communication was key to the survival of 33 miners trapped underground for 69 days. After the collapse, rescue teams drilled boreholes to establish communication with the miners. This line of communication allowed the miners to send messages to the surface about their condition, which helped rescuers develop a plan to get them out safely. Meanwhile, the miners were kept informed about rescue efforts, which boosted their morale. The ongoing exchange of information between the trapped miners and rescue teams was critical to the success of the operation.

In a different kind of emergency, the Apollo 13 mission in 1970 stands as one of the greatest examples of how communication can save lives in space. After an oxygen tank exploded during the mission, the astronauts on board were in a life-threatening situation. Communication between the crew and NASA's mission control center was crucial to solving the problem. Engineers on the ground worked with the astronauts, providing step-by-step instructions on how to repair their spacecraft and safely return to Earth. The constant back-and-forth exchange of information, combined with innovative problem-solving, allowed the crew to survive the disaster and return home.

In more localized emergencies, like tornadoes, communication often happens at the community level. In many areas prone to tornadoes, local authorities and meteorologists work closely to provide early warnings. Tornado sirens, emergency alerts, and local news broadcasts are commonly used to inform residents about incoming storms. One example comes from Joplin, Missouri, during the 2011 tornado that devastated the town. Although the tornado caused significant destruction, the early warnings and communication from the National Weather Service and local officials helped many residents take shelter in time, ultimately saving lives.

These real-life examples highlight the diverse range of communication tools and methods that can be used during emergencies. Whether it's through cutting-edge technology like early warning systems and mobile alerts, or more traditional methods like radio broadcasts and visual signals, the key is to have a reliable communication plan in place. Effective communication ensures that people receive critical information when they need it most, allowing them to take appropriate action and stay safe.

The common thread in all these cases is preparedness and the ability to quickly share information with the right people. By having multiple communication channels available—such as radios, mobile phones, social media, and community networks—people can stay informed and respond appropriately in times of crisis. These success stories reinforce the importance of practicing emergency communication plans, staying informed, and being ready to use various tools to communicate in times of need.

Analyzing Failures and Learning from Mistakes

Communication failures during emergencies can have devastating consequences, often turning manageable situations into larger crises. Analyzing these failures provides important lessons on how to improve future responses, ensuring that mistakes are not repeated. Several real-life case studies highlight the impact of poor communication and the critical lessons learned.

One notable example of communication failure occurred during Hurricane Katrina in 2005. As the hurricane approached the Gulf Coast, many government agencies and emergency response teams failed to communicate effectively with each other and the public. Confusion between local, state, and federal authorities delayed rescue efforts and the distribution of vital resources. Many people were left stranded without food, water, or shelter for days because the different levels of government had not coordinated their responses properly. One of the key lessons from this disaster was the importance of having a clear chain of command and a coordinated communication plan between agencies. In future disasters, authorities emphasized the need for better pre-established communication protocols to ensure a more efficient and unified response.

Another example comes from the 2011 Fukushima nuclear disaster in Japan. After an earthquake and tsunami severely damaged the Fukushima Daiichi nuclear plant, there was a significant delay in informing the public about the severity of the radiation leaks. The Japanese government initially downplayed the crisis, leading to confusion and mistrust among citizens. Evacuation orders were not timely, and many people were exposed to dangerous levels of radiation as a result. This case underscores the importance of transparency and timely communication during emergencies. Keeping the public informed with accurate, clear information, even if the situation is dire, can help prevent panic and allow people to take necessary precautions. The lesson here is that withholding or delaying critical information can lead to far worse outcomes than delivering bad news early on.

The 9/11 attacks in the United States also revealed significant communication failures among emergency response teams. In New York City, firefighters and police officers used different radio frequencies, which made it difficult for them to coordinate their efforts during the rescue operations. Additionally, the radio systems used by firefighters failed when the towers collapsed, leaving many responders without the ability to communicate with their teams. This lack of communication contributed to the tragic loss of life, as some emergency personnel were unaware of the imminent collapse of the towers and remained inside. One of the lessons learned from this event was the necessity for interoperable communication systems that allow all first responders to communicate seamlessly, regardless of their department or role.

In the aftermath of the 2017 Grenfell Tower fire in London, poor communication between emergency services and residents exacerbated the tragedy. Many residents of the building were told to stay in their flats, a directive based on the assumption that the fire could be contained. However, as the fire spread rapidly, this advice proved fatal for many.

Furthermore, the lack of clear communication between the firefighters on the ground and their command center hindered the overall response. This case highlights the need for flexibility in emergency communication plans. When conditions change, communication should be adaptive and responsive to new developments. Authorities must be able to issue real-time updates and change their guidance based on the evolving situation.

Another communication breakdown occurred during the 2003 European heatwave, which resulted in the deaths of over 70,000 people, particularly in France. The extreme heat overwhelmed healthcare services, and there was little public awareness about the dangers of prolonged exposure to high temperatures. Many of the victims were elderly individuals living alone, who did not receive warnings or instructions on how to protect themselves. This tragedy highlighted the importance of targeting vulnerable populations during emergencies. The lesson learned here is that communication efforts must be inclusive and consider the needs of all people, especially those who may not have access to traditional media or may be physically unable to respond to emergencies.

During the 2010 Deepwater Horizon oil spill in the Gulf of Mexico, there was a significant failure in communication between BP, the company responsible for the spill, and government agencies. Initially, BP downplayed the scale of the disaster, which delayed the federal government's response to the environmental crisis. This lack of transparency and coordination hampered cleanup efforts and allowed the spill to cause greater environmental damage. The lesson from this incident is the need for corporate accountability and honest, open communication during environmental emergencies. Government agencies and companies must work together to provide accurate information to the public and take swift action to mitigate damage.

The 2017 hurricanes Irma and Maria in Puerto Rico also exposed major communication flaws. After the storms devastated the island, much of Puerto Rico's communication infrastructure was destroyed, leaving residents and officials cut off from each other. The inability to communicate hampered rescue operations and delayed the distribution of aid. Additionally, there was poor communication between the federal government and Puerto Rican officials, which led to delays in receiving necessary resources. This disaster underscored the importance of having backup communication systems in place, such as satellite phones or alternative radio systems, to maintain communication when traditional infrastructure fails.

The 2004 Madrid train bombings also revealed communication problems that worsened the emergency response. After the attacks, there was confusion between the Spanish government and local authorities about who was responsible for the bombings. This lack of coordination led to delays in identifying the perpetrators and securing the area. Furthermore, there was insufficient communication with the public, which fueled panic and uncertainty in the immediate aftermath of the attacks. This case demonstrates the need for clear, accurate communication not only between agencies but also with the general public to prevent the spread of misinformation and fear.

One more significant case of communication failure occurred during the 2018 Camp Fire in California. Despite the rapid spread of the fire, some residents were not adequately informed about the need to evacuate. The emergency alert system failed to reach all those in the fire's path, and there were no uniform evacuation orders issued. Many people did not receive timely warnings, and as a result, the fire claimed 85 lives. The lesson here is the importance of having a robust, multi-layered alert system that can reach people through various channels, including text messages, phone calls, radio, and social media.

These case studies show that communication failures in emergencies can have tragic consequences, but they also provide valuable lessons for the future. Effective communication requires clear coordination between all parties involved, transparency in delivering information, and adaptability to changing conditions. It also highlights the importance of targeting vulnerable populations and ensuring that everyone, regardless of their situation, receives the information they need to stay safe.

By learning from these past mistakes, emergency planners and responders can improve their communication strategies and ensure that they are better prepared for future disasters. Clear, timely, and accurate communication is crucial for saving lives and minimizing the impact of emergencies.

Adapting Lessons to Your Personal Plan

Adapting the lessons learned from real-life case studies to your personal emergency communication plan can make a significant difference in how you respond during a crisis. By studying past mistakes and successes, you can strengthen your own preparedness and ensure your communication plan is effective, even in high-stress situations. Here are some practical tips to help you integrate these valuable lessons into your plan:

Establish a Clear Chain of Command

One of the most important lessons from disasters like Hurricane Katrina is the need for a clear chain of command. In your personal emergency plan, establish who will be responsible for making key decisions during a crisis. This could be yourself, a family member, or someone within your preparedness group. Ensure that everyone involved knows who to listen to and follow for updates and directions. Having a defined leader helps prevent confusion and ensures that all actions are coordinated effectively.

Prepare for Multiple Communication Methods

The 9/11 attacks and the Fukushima disaster both highlight the importance of using multiple communication methods. In your personal plan, don't rely solely on one form of communication, such as cell phones. Instead, have a backup system like two-way radios, satellite phones, or a designated meeting spot for when conventional communication methods fail. Using redundant communication tools ensures that even if one method goes down, you have alternatives to keep in touch with your loved ones or group.

Use Simple, Clear Messaging

In many emergencies, confusion and delays occur due to unclear communication. To avoid this in your own plan, ensure that all communication is clear and simple. Develop easy-to-understand messages for different scenarios, like evacuation or shelter-in-place orders. Avoid jargon or technical terms that may confuse others. Clear communication prevents misunderstandings, especially during high-pressure situations when people may not be thinking clearly.

Maintain Flexibility in Communication Plans

During the Grenfell Tower fire, authorities stuck to their initial advice even when circumstances changed, which led to tragic consequences. In your plan, build flexibility by ensuring you are ready to adapt your communication based on changing situations. Have multiple options for where to go or how to communicate and be prepared to adjust your plan as the crisis unfolds. Encourage family members or group members to stay alert and responsive to new information.

Target Vulnerable Populations

A major takeaway from the 2003 European heatwave and the Puerto Rico hurricanes is the need to communicate effectively with vulnerable populations. In your plan, make sure to account for the specific needs of children, the elderly, and individuals with disabilities. For example:

- Provide written instructions or visual cues for individuals who have difficulty hearing or understanding verbal communication.
- Assign someone responsible for checking in on vulnerable neighbors or family members during a disaster.
- Create easy-to-read materials for children to ensure they understand what to do in an emergency.

By tailoring your plan to accommodate vulnerable groups, you can ensure that everyone is included and able to respond effectively.

Develop Transparent and Honest Communication Practices

In many cases, such as the Fukushima disaster, withholding or delaying critical information worsened the crisis. In your personal communication plan, make transparency a priority. Be honest and clear about the situation, even if the news is bad. This honesty helps build trust and prevents panic. When communicating with others, avoid downplaying or exaggerating the severity of the crisis—stick to the facts and provide actionable information.

Incorporate Real-Time Updates

When a situation changes rapidly, real-time updates are crucial. In your personal plan, designate a reliable source of information, whether it's a news channel, a NOAA weather radio, or an official emergency app. Regularly check these sources during an emergency and share updates with your family or group. Assign someone to monitor these updates and relay them to others if necessary.

Practice Interoperable Communication

Similar to the communication issues during 9/11, having interoperable communication tools is key. Ensure that your communication devices (radios, phones, etc.) are compatible with those of your family, friends, and community. If possible, set up a group communication system where everyone can stay connected through a single platform. You could also explore communication apps that work offline or have emergency channels, ensuring you're all on the same page.

Plan for the Loss of Communication Infrastructure

In the aftermath of the Puerto Rico hurricanes, many people were cut off due to damaged infrastructure. When creating your plan, anticipate the possibility that cell towers, the internet, or power might go down. In this scenario, having non-digital means of communication, like walkie-talkies, signal flares, or even handwritten notes placed at a meeting point, can be lifesaving. Make sure you know how to use alternative communication devices in the event that the usual infrastructure fails.

Build a Network of Support

As the Deepwater Horizon oil spill demonstrated, lack of collaboration can slow down responses. Your personal plan should include reaching out to neighbors, friends, or community members to build a network of support. By working together, sharing resources, and staying in touch during a disaster, you can improve everyone's chances of survival. Organize periodic meetings or drills with your local community to practice communication during emergencies, strengthening these bonds.

Consider Backup Power for Communication Devices

Another key takeaway from past communication breakdowns is the importance of maintaining power to communication devices. Plan to keep extra batteries, solar chargers, or hand-crank radios available to power your devices during long-term emergencies. This ensures that you're still able to communicate even if the power grid is down.

Conduct Regular Drills and Reviews

After reviewing the failures during the Madrid train bombings, one key lesson is the importance of preparation. Conduct regular communication drills with your family or group to ensure everyone knows how to respond in an emergency. Review your communication plan periodically to update it with new technology, contacts, or methods. By practicing and reviewing your plan, you can identify any weaknesses and improve them before an actual disaster strikes.

Learn to Use Alternative Communication Methods

The lesson from the Camp Fire disaster is that emergency alert systems are not always enough. Equip yourself with knowledge of alternative communication methods, such as Morse code, hand signals, or written messages. This is especially important when verbal communication might not be possible, whether due to noisy environments, disabilities, or infrastructure failures. Learning these skills can provide additional layers of safety.

By implementing these lessons into your personal emergency communication plan, you can significantly increase your preparedness and ability to respond to disasters. Ensuring clear, adaptable, and accessible communication strategies will help protect you, your family, and your community in times of crisis. Regular practice, transparency, and the use of multiple communication methods are key to making sure your plan is reliable and effective.

CONCLUSION

The Road to Resilient Communication: Next Steps

Building resilient communication for emergencies is not only a critical part of preparedness, but also a step toward ensuring the safety and well-being of yourself, your family, and your community. Throughout this book, we have explored the many facets of emergency communication, from understanding the basics of devices and networks to mastering advanced techniques. As you reflect on the lessons shared, it's important to recognize that effective communication is the backbone of a strong emergency response.

One of the first key points discussed is the need for a well-thought-out communication plan. Having a clear, structured plan ensures that during an emergency, you know who to contact, what tools to use, and how to stay informed. You've learned the value of creating a list of contacts, including both local and out-of-area individuals, and the importance of testing your communication devices regularly. These steps form the foundation of a solid communication strategy that can be deployed when disaster strikes.

Equally essential is the idea of redundancy. Depending on just one method of communication, whether it's a phone or the internet, can be risky, especially when infrastructure fails. You've learned the importance of having backup communication options, such as radios, satellite phones, and even non-verbal methods like Morse code or hand signals. By incorporating multiple channels into your plan, you can avoid communication breakdowns and stay connected even in the most challenging situations.

The role of drills and simulations in practicing your plan cannot be understated. We covered the importance of regular practice with family members or group participants, ensuring that everyone is comfortable with the communication protocols you've established. Through drills, you can identify weak spots in your plan, improve communication flow, and strengthen your ability to respond swiftly and effectively during an emergency.

One of the more advanced topics we explored was the use of encryption and secure communication channels. In times of crisis, privacy and security become more important than ever. You've learned how to protect sensitive information and ensure that your communication remains secure from potential cyber threats. By using encrypted messages or secure networks, you can protect your information and prevent unauthorized access.

Additionally, the importance of staying informed through emergency alert systems and local networks was emphasized. Whether it's tuning into a NOAA weather radio, receiving updates through a community alert system, or responsibly using social media, being informed during an emergency can make all the difference in how you respond. Staying connected with accurate and timely information allows you to make well-informed decisions that ensure the safety of those around you.

Special attention was also given to overcoming communication barriers. Whether it's dealing with language differences, communicating with vulnerable populations like children or the elderly, or addressing disabilities, you've learned how to ensure that your message is clear and accessible to everyone. Emergencies affect all individuals differently, and being mindful of these challenges in your communication plan makes it more inclusive and effective.

As you move forward, the most important takeaway is action. Emergency communication isn't something to think about only when disaster strikes; it's something to plan, prepare, and practice regularly. Take the knowledge you've gained and start by reviewing your current emergency communication plan, or if you don't have one yet, begin building it. Equip yourself with the right tools, familiarize yourself with communication networks, and involve your family, friends, and community in your efforts.

Ultimately, the goal is not just to survive a disaster, but to thrive in the face of it. By ensuring that your communication is resilient, adaptable, and secure, you are laying the groundwork for a more prepared and safer future. The road to resilient communication starts with small steps, but each action you take strengthens your overall preparedness. Stay proactive, continue learning, and remember that in any emergency, communication is your lifeline.

www.ingramcontent.com/pod-product-compliance
Lightning Source LLC
Chambersburg PA
CBHW052140220526
45471CB00004B/1451